Back Chairs. —

P9-EDR-540

Act of Parliml.

M. Darly Sculp.

Collecting
ANTIQUE
FURNITURE

Collecting
ANTIQUE

FURNITURE

Peter Johnson

Galahad Books

New York

Published by Galahad Books
a division of A & W Promotional Book Corporation
95 Madison Avenue, New York, NY 10016

Library of Congress Catalog Card No. 76–11591
ISBN 0–88365–367–2

© Copyright The Hamlyn Publishing Group Limited 1976
London · New York · Sydney · Toronto
Astronaut House, Feltham,
Middlesex, England

Phototypeset in England by
Keyspools Limited, Golborne, Lancashire
Printed in Hong Kong by
Toppan Printing Co. (H.K.) Limited

1 *half-title page* An Elizabethan court
cupboard, so named from the French *court*–short.
The three recessed panels in the upper
section are inlaid with holly and bog oak.

2 *title page* The gate-leg table came in
many forms. American makers added the
distinctive touch of butterfly wings–solid,
shaped supports opening beneath
the flaps. This version is in English yew wood,
has a double-gate action and dates
from the 17th century.

Contents

Love
has no price

In the darkness of a storage cupboard under the stairs of a modest English country house the furniture specialist from one of London's major auction rooms was taking a last look around before completing a routine valuation. The beam of his flashlight played on a dusty item of furniture tucked away amid boxes, buckets and brooms. It was a moment which was to earn the householder a substantial windfall. 'Do you mind if I have a look at this?' asked the valuer. 'Not at all,' said the householder. 'It's an old cabinet that has been there for years.'

In the daylight the 'old cabinet' emerged as a Chinese export bureau cabinet from the 18th century, constructed of lacquer panels. Diagonal stripes of gold lacquer on a black ground decorated the surface, together with painted flowers and fruit. The lower section with its drawers and fall front writing desk was surmounted by an elegant upper part with mirrored cupboard doors, the whole being topped by a shaped pediment and gilded bird carving. Certainly not the greatest saleroom find of the 1970s, but important enough to arouse international interest when it came under the auctioneer's hammer some weeks later and fell to the highest bidder at £11,500. Its last owner was delighted of course, and as he pocketed the proceeds of the auction sale he confessed: 'I was wondering what to do with that old cabinet and, believe it or not, I was seriously thinking of breaking it up and turning the base into a coffee table.'

Now I am not for one moment suggesting that a discovery such as this is common. Sadly most of us know that we have nothing more than brooms in the broom cupboard. It illustrates, however, two important aspects of the modern phenomenon of collecting antiques. Firstly, 'finds' do happen. (And, after all, the joy of serendipity is a major stimulus to the man or woman who, with a modest amount to spend, trawls the local antique shops, just as it is to the millionaire collector who fishes in more specialised and expensive waters.) The second point about the discovery of the Chinese cabinet is that it illustrates the background of constantly rising prices, which is so much a part of the furniture collecting scene. Many excellent books have been written on antique furniture. All too often, however, the authors have fought shy of discussing prices as though money were anathema to the cabinetmakers of old. Thomas Chippendale put a price—and a high one at that—on his labour; if Thomas Sheraton lived and died a pauper it was not for want of trying; and Nicholas Disbrowe, the English emigrant from Saffron Walden, 'cutte and jouned' for thirty-odd years in Hartford, Connecticut, without ever learning to read or write, but he was not above coining an honest penny from his American colonial clients.

Having said all that, however, no book on furniture collecting can pretend to be a price guide, particularly in these days of heady inflation, without being outdated as soon as it is off the presses. Hardly a day goes by without the salerooms of New York, London, Geneva or Paris notching up yet another record for a piece of furniture. As international money markets fluctuate and once-trusted stocks and bonds lose their shine, more and more money is put into moveable objects of value. New vogues in collecting appear. New markets open. With the intervention of the Japanese in the collecting scene of the 1970s we have seen immense price rises in many things oriental, a move also influenced by China's rapprochement with the West. Within a few months of the broom closet Chinoiserie appearing in the daylight and going for a mandarin's ransom at Phillips, Britain's third largest firm of auctioneers, it was the turn of Christie's, along the road, to make headlines with an astounding example of appreciation in the value of a fine piece of furniture—again in the Chinese style which has attracted some of the best cabinetmakers of history.

Attributed to Thomas Chippendale, Britain's great craftsman, whose name has come to represent a whole style and period of 18th-century furniture, a bedroom commode or chest of drawers was made around 1770 for Harewood House in Yorkshire. Its outstanding features are the superb panels veneered with Chinese black and gold lacquer and portraying scenes of buildings and islands. Harmony and symmetry are present in the gently bowed front and concave sides. It is a piece fit for an aristocrat, with its drawer containing a magnificent set of vermilion fitted boxes and a support for a mirror at which a lady could attend to her toilet. I have no record to show the price of this masterpiece when it came from Chippendale's hand in the 1770s. What we do know is that it came up for auction in 1951 when it was sold by the Harewoods and fetched £483. Just twenty-two years later it clocked up a magnificent £32,550 in the same auction rooms. Beat that on the stock market if you can!

That's fine, you might say, but we are collecting furniture *today*, and where do we start if we don't have that sort of money? The answer is: do not be afraid of the big, headline-making news which pours daily from the international salerooms. Every auction room, quite rightly, boasts about its record-breaking prices. The better material the auctioneers attract, the more money they are going to make. But for every world record they shatter, whether it be for furniture, porcelain, silver or pictures, they are just as dependent on the mass of good lower and middle range antiques which are more likely

Numbers in the margin refer to illustrations

3 An auction room specialist came across this bureau cabinet in the broom closet of an English country house. The owner had no idea of its value. At auction it made a cool £11,500. It was fashioned to contemporary English designs and lacquered in black and gold in China in the 18th century.

to be destined for ordinary, discerning homes rather than the great museums of the world or the palatial residences of millionaire collectors. In fact, most of the leading salerooms estimate that 80 per cent of their lots sell for under £150 each—let's say under $300. And it is in this field that scope for the collector has widened over the past few years as the result of some interesting developments.

Awareness of antiques—coupled with the astronomically soaring values of practically anything made before the end of the 18th century—has led to the advancement of time frontiers. Periods which were unacceptable in the 'trade' or to the discerning collector of the inter-war years are now valid fields for collecting. In Britain many authors have written off the major part of the 19th century as though Queen Victoria's accession to the throne in 1837 and the consequent development of the machine age ruled out any hope of worthwhile furniture being made after that date. A commentator on the Victorians wrote at the turn of the century of 'the most tasteless ineptitude in nearly every branch of art', and his words reflect attitudes which have long robbed the 19th century of its fair dues.

More modern frontiers have always been accepted in America, where periods and styles tended to trail their relative movements in Europe, as the chart on pages 10–11 shows. Paradoxically, this absence of trans-atlantic synchronisation has produced some fascinating American furniture as the design style of one era lapped over the climate of thought of a later age. No better example is to be found than in the Windsor chair, with its half-dozen American variations on an essentially English design, which has always been deemed 'country style' in its land of origin and has therefore not been the target of as much experimentation as in America.

Thus we find that the 19th century—call it Victorian or what you will—is 'in'. Leading salerooms now hold regular sales of Victorian furniture and other artifacts. The world's major antiques fairs are gradually easing their datelines. The 1920s have their adherents, as does the 'Art Deco' of the 1930s. Not so long ago a chrome, formica and perspex jukebox of 1952 vintage made its appearance in the hallowed halls of Sotheby's. We hear much talk of 'tomorrow's antiques', whatever that may mean.

It is not the role of this book to tread into such late collecting areas of the 20th century, except to indicate briefly how movements such as the English Arts and Crafts of the 1880s led to the development of Art Nouveau and functionalism. A serious attempt will be made, however, to explore the much neglected 19th

century. Availability is an important stimulus to collecting, and this quality, among others, is present in the field of 19th-century furniture. In contrast, there are few objects of furniture in the world to rival a small ($14\frac{1}{2}$ inches wide) *table à café*, mounted with a Sèvres porcelain top and made in the days of Louis XV of France (1715–1774). Its beauty of craftsmanship, its rarity and its provenance were enough to put it in the £100,000-plus class when it appeared in a London saleroom, to be sold from the collection of the late Sydney J. Lamon, of New York City. At that price, there can be a limited number of potential buyers for such a piece. In fact, the Iranian collector who paid £115,000 for the table said afterwards: 'Love has no price.' Fortunately, however, between the products of the lush patronage of kings and the furniture needs of 19th-century Europe and America lies a rich, varied and rewarding ground for the collector. And that, basically, is what collecting furniture is all about.

Oak makes a comeback

The time chart on pages 10–11 is an attempt to guide the reader through the complicated maze of interrelated movements and styles which have affected furniture design. I have taken the accepted division of English cabinetmaking periods as a basic yardstick, not through any chauvinistic belief that the world owes all to England, but because such a device is expedient in explaining the trends of history.

There have been fairly clearly defined ages of furniture design since the Renaissance, that flowering of thought in Europe which in the 15th and 16th centuries ushered in classical ideas of Greece and Rome after the Middle Ages. These can be simplified in England (with a certain amount of overlapping) as the ages of oak (up to and including the mid 17th century), walnut (late 17th and early 18th) and mahogany (most of the 18th from about 1720).

Early American cabinetmakers understandably employed local woods such as maple, fruit and nut woods and pine as well as their softer version of the oak of old England. By the 16th century the Dutch and Flemish, with their merchant sea-going traditions, were experimenting with exotic oriental woods. And in Italy, where stylishness and cutting *la bella figura* were all-important, walnut was most in evidence, but various regions had their favourite choice of wood; thus Venice, denied the better woods such as walnut because of their expense, was renowned for lacquer, Lombardy made do with olive and Tuscany turned to its fruit and nut trees.

It is ironic that oak, one of the oldest of woods in this history should have made only fairly recently a remarkable impact on the furniture-collecting scene; during the first half of the 1970s in fact. Almost completely out of fashion for many years, the heavy, oak look of the 17th century came back into favour about the start of the 1970s. The old sales books of Dowell's, the Edinburgh auctioneers, list a Cromwellian oak refectory table on spirally turned legs, dating from the 1650s, as selling for eleven pounds and sixpence in 1904. A table of similar date and proportions, if slightly differing style, has realised £400 in London some 70 years later.

It seemed that oak furniture of ample size had no place in our modern style of living, with smaller rooms demanding pieces of scaled-down proportions. However, the growing popularity of the second home in the country and an increasing acceptance of the more primitive 'country look' in furniture have once again put oak on the map. Of course it would be naive to think that these were the only factors in oak's resurgence. Shrewd

investors perceived in the late 1960s that old oak was ludicrously cheap compared with walnut and mahogany. It was only a matter of time before the better oak began to disappear until today you will find good early pieces only at the highly specialised dealer's. Therefore if you seek a bargain in oak you must look farther afield. The remotest country areas have been well combed by the dealers. Only a dreamer would think he still has a chance of finding for a handful of pounds in an English or Welsh village an oak dresser, or even a highly desirable dresser base, being the lower section containing two or three drawers on which the upper part, the shelves, stood. Similarly, we have seen the once-prevalent kas (Dutch *kast*–cupboard) become a rarity in the rural areas of New York and New Jersey. This massive oak construction, often with ebonised or painted panels on its four cupboard doors and standing on bulbous bun feet, was beloved of Dutch and Flemish housewives who used it for storing linen and other household goods from the 17th century onwards. As Dutch merchants settled New Amsterdam, which was to become New York, the kas, either as an object or as an idea, was imported into America and became a common feature of furnishing in that area right through to the 19th century. Its rarity has now put it in an expensive bracket in East Coast antiques markets.

Therefore we must look to later centuries for available oak. 18th-century oak has risen in price commensurately with the 17th century. And again there is not a wealth of it about; after all, by that time oak was competing with the fashionable calls of walnut, mahogany and satinwood. So the collector must turn to the much maligned 19th century, from which some sensible, well made oak furniture is available. There are many traps for the inexperienced, for this was a time when faking and deceitful reproduction were rife, but with the right amount of care good 'buys' can still be found. Not long ago I managed to buy in a London general antique shop an unpretentious but sound late Victorian davenport in oak. The davenport, not to be confused with the American sofa-bed or low table of the same name, is a derivation of the small writing desk said to have been ordered by a Captain Davenport from Gillow's, the English furnituremakers, in the 1790s. It usually has four drawers opening from one side, with false drawers on the other. A sloping top is lifted to reveal a compartment for papers, usually fitted with two small drawers. At the top and back of the slope is an opening section for pens and ink, and in the more sophisticated example

4 This Charles II oak dresser base measures six feet in length and represents a type of furniture—much neglected until the early 1970s—now in great demand. The front legs are baluster-turned. As with much large furniture of the time, however, the back legs remain plain supports as they were meant to stand against the wall out of full view.

5 Oliver Cromwell is reputed to have taken communion at this table when it was in use at a Hertfordshire Congregational church in the 17th century. Its simple oak lines are relieved only by the turned baluster legs on bun feet.

The Ages of English Furniture

The Age of Oak

ELIZABETH I	1558–1603

Massive carving, becoming more elaborate. Bun feet. Oak chests with linen-fold panelling in the form of folded cloth. Court cupboards. By mid 17th century oak dressers in their full glory and gate-leg tables have arrived. Chests and other furniture have become more decorative. Growth of inlay and the upholstered chair. Complicated devices for woodturning introduced, so that the spiral turned leg could be made. Chests placed on stands; drawers arrive.

Best buy for modern day small collectors: oak 'coffin' stools.

JAMES I	1603–1625
CHARLES I	1625–1649
COMMONWEALTH	1649–1660

The Age of Walnut

CHARLES II	1660–1685
JAMES II	1685–1688
WILLIAM & MARY	1689–1702

Foreign influence shows in marquetry and cane-back chairs. Cabriole leg arrives around 1680. Windsor chairs by 1690. Claw and ball foot 1700. Queen Anne period: dignity and proportion, bureau bookcases, card tables, lacquer cabinets. Architectural furniture for great houses.

Best buy: Windsor chairs.

ANNE	1702–1714
GEORGE I	1714–1727

The Age of Mahogany

GEORGE II	1727–1760

Chippendale 1718–1779 (*Director* published 1754): fine-proportioned 'square-look' chairs on straight and cabriole legs; also Chinese and Gothic. Hepplewhite's *Guide* published 1788. Sheraton 1751–1806 (*Drawing Book* published 1791): makes much use of satinwood, fine inlay, classical styles, sabre legs. Sofas develop and the sofa table appears in numbers; davenport desks; convex mirrors. Greek, Roman and Egyptian influence and some neo-Gothicism. *Best buy: Georgian swing frame toilet mirrors.*

GEORGE III	1760–1820
REGENCY	*1811–1820*
GEORGE IV	1820–1830
WILLIAM IV	1830–1837

The Victorian Age

Rosewood and mahogany. Balloon-back and heavily upholstered chairs, including button-backs. Elaborately carved sideboards. Whatnots and parlour tables. Ebonised furniture. Dressing tables by 1850. Iron furniture–brass and iron beds from 1850. Bamboo and papier mâché. Arts and Crafts movement introduces the organic line in 1880s. Throughout, many reproduced styles–Eastern, Sheraton, Chippendale, Louis, Elizabethan etc.

Best buys: Davenports, button-backs, brass beds.

VICTORIA	1837–1901

Early Colonial and 17th Century

e

Local oak and much pine used. Wainscot (or waggon board) furniture. Brewster and Carver chairs. Massachusetts and Connecticut are the principal furniture making areas. In 1639 Nicholas Disbrowe, cabinetmaker, settles in Hartford. Hadley chests and court cupboards on typical American lines. Sunflower and tulip chests still carry a resemblance to the Tudor rose. Around 1680 Philadelphia emerges as important furniture centre.

Although France has a long and distinguished furniture heritage going back several centuries, the chart concentrates on the major periods of the 18th century, which had the greatest effect on contemporary and 19th-century English and American furniture.

18th Century

Dutch kas (cupboard) common in New York and New Jersey. Maple, walnut and burr walnut veneers popular. Cabriole leg from 1720 onwards, claw and ball foot from 1750. Rise of Rhode Island block front furniture 1760–1780. Chippendale style from 1760. Highboys and secretaries appear. Philadelphia is supreme. War of Independence 1776–1783.

f

Louis XIV 1643–1715 *Baroque*

The king's love of sumptuousness leads to magnificence at court and high patronage. Large, masculine, Baroque pieces. Tables, armoires, cabinets on architectural lines. Versailles built 1661–1687. Grands salons with furniture designed for room settings. In 1685 the Protestants lose their protection by the revocation of the Edict of Nantes, and many fine craftsmen flee to Netherlands and England.

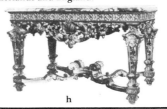

h

Louis XV 1715–1774 *Rococo*

Feminine Rococo after masculine Baroque. Petits salons. Straight lines give way to bombé curves. Influence of Madame De Pompadour and Madame Du Barry. Exotic woods used.

i

Louis XVI 1774–1792

Straight lines return. The 'boudoir' look in interior decoration. Tulip, rose, holly, laburnum and other woods. Revolution in 1789. In the ensuing Reign of Terror, much fine furniture destroyed or disposed of.

Empire and 19th Century

Death to Rococo. First Empire returns to the classical line. Greek, Roman and Egyptian symbolism. 1798 Napoleon in Egypt. Fine, rich mahogany plentiful.

j

Federal and 19th Century

Hepplewhite and French influence shows in 1780s. Classical style carries over to 19th century. New York, Salem, Baltimore grow in importance 1800–1830. Duncan Phyfe (1768–1854) strongly influenced by Sheraton, classical Greek and Egyptian: animal heads and feet. Birch, satinwood, paint and gilt complement mahogany and rosewood. From 1825 onward Hitchcock chair ousts Windsor in popularity. Shaker furniture. Through the 19th century French Empire is followed by many styles such as Rococo, Gothic, Renaissance, etc. As in Britain, mass production takes over in furniture.

g

Key to illustrations
a See plate 4.   b See plate 15.   c See plate 39.   d Balloon-back chair.
e American Colonial 'butterfly' gate-leg table.   f American block front chest of drawers.   g See plate 79.   h Carved and gilt Louis XIV table, *Musée des Arts Décoratifs, Paris*.   i See plate 30.   j French mahogany writing table of about 1810, *Musée de Malmaison*.

6 Holland produced this massive oak kas (Dutch *kast*—cupboard) in the 17th century. The style was much followed by New York and New Jersey descendants of the first Dutch settlers of New Amsterdam. American versions were once common. Now they command high prices from collectors.

you will find a pierced brass gallery and a mechanically rising section of fine workmanship. The more expensive davenports are in walnut or are ebonised—stained black to resemble ebony—and some, worth five or six times as much as my oak desk, are illustrated in the chapter on desks. Mine has a light and attractive interior in bird's-eye maple wood and was a bargain at £60. In its first year it had already appreciated some 40 per cent according to well watched auction prices. Acknowledgments to my humble davenport are given not because it claims to be a connoisseur's piece, but because it is an example of an honest antique—or near antique—which still can be bought fairly inexpensively.

By the time Elizabeth I came to the throne in England in 1558 life was becoming more refined, and the wealthy were demanding much more comfort in their surroundings. The oak chest—in its earlier form simply a box with a lid—had been the principal means of storage for

linen, plate or other items. Before the 16th century it was to undergo various changes in Europe. Just as the Italian *cassone* or chest became the *cassapanca* (a seat with arms and back), so the English chest sprouted high back and arms to become the draught-excluding settle. A walnut *cassapanca* from the early 17th century exhibits rich carvings of armorial designs, leaves, scrolls and urns, and its inherent hardness would later be softened by cushions. The English woodcarver, taught by foreign craftsmen imported to decorate the homes of the wealthy, was encouraged to fashion elaborate creations such as half-human half-monster figures which supported buffets, used for the storage of utensils and the service of meals. Table legs and bedposts grew into huge acorn-shaped constructions. In the choir stalls of Henry VII's chapel at Westminster Abbey was fashioned typical woodcarving of the period, which often embodied the linen-fold pattern. In contrast to the grotesque, this was a stylised form representing in wood a folded napkin, much used on oak chests whose main function was the storage of linen. The linen-fold pattern was popular through Elizabeth's reign and after her death in 1603.

Furniture design complemented architectural and interior decoration as the fruits of a dynamic sea-going policy came home to 16th-century England. The living quarters of the rich reflected the contemporary affluence. The best of the woodcarver's art can be seen at Hampton Court, Henry VIII's splendid palace in what are now the inner suburbs of London. In the centre of London, Middle Temple Hall was adorned with a sumptuous carved oak screen, and the builders of nearby Gray's Inn employed the growing skills of the Elizabethan carver with effect. Great manor houses were created in Oxfordshire, Lincolnshire, Norfolk and elsewhere, many of which are open to the public. One of the houses built during the English Renaissance is Sutton Place, near Guildford, 30 miles from London, in which American oil tycoon Paul Getty made his home four centuries later. The house, with its superb furniture of several periods, is open to sightseers at certain times of the year, and visitors should enquire from their travel agent.

High on the list of any antiques-conscious visitor to London, however, must be the Victoria and Albert Museum which, apart from individual examples of furniture of all ages, houses some completely preserved room settings. In a museum which boasts so many riches, it is difficult to pick out individual items of furniture. Nevertheless there is an Elizabethan carved oak bedstead which is astonishing in its proportions, being 7 feet 11 inches long and 5 feet 8 inches wide. These dimensions, particularly the length, are remarkable when considering that the average Elizabethan was of much less stature than the 20th-century Englishman. In recent years planners of a replica Shakespearian Globe Theatre

on the south bank of the Thames had to revise their seating design fundamentally. They had wanted the tiers of benches to follow exactly the dimensions and spacing of the Bard's day. They discovered, however, that this was impossible as a 20th-century audience needed more leg-room, the Elizabethan's thigh bone being on average 2 inches shorter than that of his modern compatriot.

The giant four-poster bed apart, such facts raise an interesting point for collectors of furniture of these times. Oak implies massiveness, but despite the robustness of style in which the craftsman had to work (and remember, too, that his chairs had to accommodate capacious dresses), there is a proportion inherent in 16th- and early 17th-century furniture which escapes the modern copyist. This is the proportion scaled to the size of the contemporary human figure. Testing a 17th-century stool for size will quickly illustrate how the human frame has increased in stature over the centuries, and the discomfort of many early chairs will be apparent.

Voluminous clothing went far to ease the hardness of contemporary furniture. However, the upholstered chair had arrived late in Elizabeth's reign and was well established by the early 17th century. Style went along

9

8 The Italian *cassapanca* of the 16th century developed from the *cassone* or chest by assuming back and arms. This richly carved specimen in walnut once graced the home of an Italian nobleman.

with the growing demand for comfort. The court cupboard, which had been a simple storage and service unit with three open shelves, assumed cupboard doors and intricate carving. Cabinets, a big step in sophistication from the simple oak chests of earlier days, were sometimes decorated with inlay, thin pieces of contrasting woods, ivory, bone or mother-of-pearl set into the carcase wood to make patterns.

Inlay and its cousin marquetry were to be much used in the 18th century when improved techniques permitted the use of flimsier cuts than the one-sixteenth of an inch thickness common in earlier days. As distinct from inlay, marquetry involves the use of a veneer of fine woods, glued as a 'coat' over the entire surface of the carcase to form a pattern of contrasting shades or grains. The technique was much used by the Dutch and Flemish cabinetmakers who impressed Europe with their skills in the first half of the 17th century. Exotic materials, shipped home from the East by merchant venturers, stimulated the Dutch interest in marquetry, a technique

which achieves a strikingly impressive effect from what is essentially a simple process.

First, slices of veneer thickness are sawn from squared and planed logs of two different woods. Veneer A is clamped to veneer B and the two materials are cut simultaneously in simple or intricate designs. Two complete designs are obtained, one being the reverse of the other. In one case the basic pattern is in material A and the ground work in material B, and vice versa. Thus in marquetry, unlike fret, nothing is thrown away.

Dutch cabinetmakers' preference was for fantastic designs of flowers and foliage in profusion, urns and grotesque figures. Emigré ideas were responsible for similar marquetry styles, tempered by English restraint, after William of Orange came to the throne of England in 1689. At the same time, inter-relation of influences produced magnificent examples of marquetry furniture under the patronage of the French court, where the style reached its high point in the creations of André-Charles Boulle (1642–1732), renowned for his marquetry

9 Simple and dependable, a 17th-century oak stool of a type made on both sides of the Atlantic. One test for age is to look for scuff marks on the stretchers which unite the legs —telling evidence of use over the centuries.

of brass and tortoiseshell. Examples of his art command astronomical prices today. It was much imitated by English 19th-century cabinetmakers whose efforts are naturally nearer the pockets of the average collector. True Boulle is to be found only in the private collections of the very wealthy in Europe and America and in such internationally known museums as the Louvre in Paris and the V & A and the Wallace Collection in London. Before leaving the subject of marquetry, mention should be made of the style known as parquetry, a term applied to veneer of angular-cut pieces, arranged in a geometrical pattern and usually found on large cabinets or on panels of early longcase clocks.

Despite the introduction of inlay and the appearance of oriental styles, the woodcarver's influence was strong throughout the 17th century. New skills were arising, however, and improved lathes allowed more complicated turned wooden supports for furniture. The spiral twist leg had its day and was to be seen universally in chair and table legs, as decorations on cabinets and as pillars 10 flanking the dials of longcase clocks.

Splendid furniture was made in the counties of England and Wales as the fortunes of country folk moved forward steadily if not as ostentatiously as those of their town cousins. The Yorkshire chair, with its open arcaded back and two crescent-shaped cross rails, was born of the late 17th century, and similar ones were made in East Anglia and the Midlands of England. The Welsh dresser (with its English counterpart) was in its 121, 124 full glory. A remarkable example has made a record price of £1,300 at the auction rooms of John Francis & Son in Carmarthen, Wales. Until its record-breaking appearance, £500 would have been considered high for a Welsh dresser. Within one hour of being bought by a dealer the dresser changed hands again. The underbidder, a Welsh private collector, backed his convictions with his cash and offered £1,600 to the dealer, who accepted. The collector wanted to prevent the dresser being exported—to England! Thus nationalism affects the soaring economics of furniture collecting.

A society which had moved away from communal feeding at long oak tables, placed in the great halls, accepted the introduction of the gate-leg table with enthusiasm. By mid 17th century this design was firmly established. It was convenient, being of a form and size to be pushed against a wall for use as a side table until it was needed to seat six or eight people for dinner, when the flap on one or both sides would be raised and the gates pulled out to support the extension.

London fashions inevitably took time to reach other parts of England and longer to reach the new American colonies where difficulties of pioneer life and the Puritan *mores* of New England had a sobering effect on design. In addition, an immigrant people occupied with wresting a life from the wilderness, had little time for

15

10 A Dutch walnut side table of about 1700, with typical tapering twist legs. The carved apron below the drawer is a feature which appeared in Dutch-influenced furniture in New York up to a century after this table was made.
11 Boulle work, fine inlay of brass and tortoiseshell after the renowned French cabinetmaker André-Charles Boulle (1642–1732), decorates this 19th-century version of a lady's writing desk. It is typical of much 'styling' from earlier times in 19th-century England.

the niceties of documentation; so the historian finds a scarcity of written information describing early American-made furniture and often has to turn to invoices and wills. What was long thought to be the earliest *signed* piece of American furniture is a Hadley chest (named from the town of its origin in Massachusetts), now in the Bayou Bend Collection at Houston, Texas. It is a carved front chest with two drawers underneath and bears a label purporting to be that of Nicholas Disbrowe, the immigrant from Essex who settled in Hartford, Connecticut, in 1639. The inscription reads: 'Mary Allyns Chist, cutte and jouned by Nich. Disbrowe.' The authenticity of the inscription, if not the antiquity of the chest, is disputed on the grounds that Disbrowe was illiterate. Even though someone else might have inscribed his work for him, the sceptics also point out that

the letters S lack serifs, further evidence that the label was added later than the 17th century.

With the Restoration of the monarchy in 1660 and Charles II installed on the throne, furniture took on a fresh colour after the sobering climate of the English Commonwealth. The Queen, Catherine of Braganza, introduced fashions from her native Portugal, itself influenced by its possessions in India and the East. The high backed chair, often with seat and back of cane or finely tooled leather, became popular and later assumed patterned upholstery, as it was doing throughout Europe. The stretcher connecting the front legs of a chair was raised or moved back, being no longer needed to support the sitter's feet as carpets and wooden floors ousted rushes and cold stone. Elaborate carving made the stretcher a feature of ornamentation in its own right

17

12 A Thomas Chippendale bedroom commode made for Harewood House in Yorkshire around 1770. In 1951 it realised £483 at auction. Twenty-two years later the price was up to £32,550.

13 The finest furniture the world has known came from France in the 18th century. Such an example is this delicate *table à café* with its superb Sèvres porcelain top and cabriole legs.

until it was to vanish almost wholly with the establishment in fashion of the cabriole leg.

Appearing from France around 1680, the cabriole leg really took hold in England when Dutch influences were nourished in the reign of William and Mary (1689–1702). After that time it developed into a principal feature of the 18th century's great age of walnut. The cabriole, or bandy, support is said to represent the leg of a leaping goat and its description comes from the Latin (*caper* – goat) via Italian and French. By the reign of the dual monarchs another Netherlands importation was on the scene – the claw and ball foot, brought from the East by the Dutch and representing the Chinese symbol of the dragon's claw holding a pearl. Although the year 1700 saw the claw and ball foot in use in England, American craftsmen of New England were not employing the style extensively until nearly 50 years later. Similarly, 17th-century Connecticut had nourished the typical sunflower and tulip chests of the Hartford area, named for their carved motifs. Sunflower it may be in the books; some observers, however, claim it was a nostalgic throwback to the Tudor rose of England, and yet another instance of the way American styles trailed European.

The isolation of the American colonists from the artistic 'happenings' in Europe was by no means entirely a debit, as Australia was later to discover in its own experience. Typical American styles developed early, such as the simple Carver and Brewster chairs, named after two leaders of the Massachusetts Bay colony, both rather uncomfortable, spindle-back chairs. For the next two centuries there were exciting movements in American furniture, often brought about because an English or European fashion of, say, thirty or even fifty years earlier was being developed in a new climate of thought on the western side of the Atlantic.

But for sheer magnitude of events in architectural and furniture design we must look to France in the reign of Louis XIV (1643–1715). This was the age of Baroque, masculine magnificence which took its cue from the unrivalled splendours of the court. It saw the building of Versailles, which took six years and at one time employed 36,000 men and 6,000 horses. Tables, cabinets, chairs were on the grand scale, employing the talents of such masters as Boulle, specialists in gilding, artists in

14 As wooden floors and carpets ousted cold stone and rushes, there was no longer any need for a low-placed stretcher on which the sitter would rest his feet. Thus we find in this late 17th-century South German beechwood chair a front stretcher which has

moved considerably higher and become a decorative feature in its own right.
15 A chair with a cabriole leg with claw and ball foot, a style which came to England around the end of the 17th century. Dutch craftsmen borrowed the motif from China.

16 Cane was much used in back and seat panels by English chairmakers in the second half of the 17th century. The motif of carved walnut scrolls is used all over this chair, even down to the feet.

51 lacquer and sculptors of marble. Ormolu—bronze or brass mounts worked into designs of figures, animals and plants—decorated huge pieces which were designed to be seen in the harmony of complete room settings, themselves sumptuous concepts gaining additional richness from tapestries, carpets, silks from Italy and Lyons, and superb porcelain.

In 1685 Louis revoked the Edict of Nantes under which Protestants had received a measure of protection in Catholic France. It was to prove artistically beneficial to both England and Holland. French Protestant cabinet-makers, glassworkers and weavers fled to England and set up in business, and their talents were eagerly welcomed by the increasingly prospering upper classes. Grinling Gibbons, a poor woodcarver immigrant from the Netherlands, was discovered working on a carving of Tintoretto's *Crucifixion*. Such was the efficiency of patronage that he was quickly taken from his Thames-side workshop at Deptford and introduced to Sir

Christopher Wren and Samuel Pepys, and later to the royal family. Wren used his talents in the rebuilt St Paul's Cathedral and in other fine churches and houses, and Gibbons ended his days in 1721 as Master Carver to George I on a retainer of one shilling and sixpence a day, comfortable pay in those days.

The century was closing in a climate of exciting economic and artistic movements. The growth of literacy had led to the birth of the slope front bureau, at first a chest of drawers with a writing section forming the upper part, which in turn was to develop into the quintessentially English bureau bookcase. Display cabinets made an appearance to meet the new fashion for collecting china. For the first time there were card tables as gaming became a popular pastime and vice. Above all, the cabinetmakers had turned to walnut, softer than oak, available in quantity from the maturing forests (and later imported from Virginia) and ideal for the flowing lines and curves of current furniture fashion.

The 18th century
Walnut and mahogany

In 1702 Queen Anne started a twelve-year reign of crucial importance to the British royal succession, a reign which gave history books the names of famous battles like Blenheim, Ramillies and Malplaquet and which was dominated militarily by John Churchill, Duke of Marlborough. Significantly, however, a modern American author, in a collection of royal jingles of England, opens her epitaph to Anne with a verse which, while not claiming to be great poetry, is appropriate to the context of this book.

Anne was a queen who founded an Age.
In all the antique shops she's really the rage.
A Queen Anne sofa or a Queen Anne chair,
A Queen Anne table and fine silverware,
And Queen Anne lace in the drygoods store.
And last but not least, there was Queen Anne's war.

All of which seems to point up the old adage that Queen Anne is remembered for her cabriole legs. Predictably, the period known as Queen Anne lasted in colonial America until at least 15 years after her death. In the home country the trend towards more comfort was continuing with the tall chair giving way to one of moderate height, shaped to fit the sitter's back. Simple proportions and dignity of style marked much Queen Anne furniture. Chairs and tables adopted the cabriole leg. Splats—the central vertical part of an open back—were often flat or of vase or baluster shape. An American development was the banister-back chair, which retained the cane seat of its European ancestor, but embodied four spindles in the high back. These spindles were usually rounded on the front, flat on the back. There were also slat back chairs, with four or five horizontal slats, and painted a dull black. England saw more interesting use of veneers, including burr walnut, a veneer cut from the malformations on trees, and the similar oyster veneer, obtained from transverse layers of the bough or root. The latter was usually of laburnum or walnut and much used on table tops and chests of drawers.

On both sides of the Atlantic—and throughout the 18th century—the card table was having its vogue, more noticeably in England, uninhibited by the *mores* of the Founding Fathers. As trade between Europe and China grew in volume, lacquered cabinets were imported through Holland into England. Some cabinets and long-cases for clocks were fashioned by English cabinet-makers and shipped out to China in vessels engaged in

the tea trade, to return three years later superbly lacquered by Chinese specialists. Chinoiserie was to make frequent claims on popularity throughout the 18th and 19th centuries. English attempts at lacquerwork—or japanning as it was called—were usually dismal failures. Various American cabinetmakers in the now dominant centres of Philadelphia and Boston (and also elsewhere) tried their hands at japanning with no more success. There, it was the turn of the carver to come into his own again with somewhat restrained decoration appearing on the knees of cabriole legs and on the crest rails of chair backs. The English bureau bookcase—thirty or more years later it became the American secretary—established itself in elegant proportions which often eluded the aspirations of Continental copyists.

Transatlantic influence was not always in one direction. A marble topped side table from the time of George I—who began the Hanoverian succession after the death of Anne in 1714—was recently auctioned in London. It was decorated with gilt gesso, chalk worked into paste with parchment size, hardened then carved in low relief and gilded (sometimes called the poor man's ormolu). What was remarkable, however, was the fact that the legs were headed by carved masks of American Indians. In the absence of transatlantic provenance, it may be assumed that some traveller having returned from the Colonies was imbued with the frontier spirit and commissioned the design from an English maker. The table's American flavour undoubtedly contributed to its auction price of 1,150 guineas (Christie's, founded in 1776 not long after this table was made, preferred until 1976 to cling charmingly to the old-fashioned monetary unit of £1.05). Any Colonial or Federal pieces which appear in overseas salerooms are snapped up as eagerly as in New York or Los Angeles. On the other hand, although early American furniture is rare and costly, it is remarkable how much actually exists, considering that now-enormous cities were small settlements in the 18th century. Pace-setting Philadelphia, for instance (population over 4,800,000 in 1970), was a town of 12,500 inhabitants in 1750.

Chauvinistic supporters of America's furniture heritage have from time to time claimed that the earliest use of mahogany was in the Colonies. The claim is based on the generally accepted opinion that England's age of mahogany opened about 1720 whereas New York and Philadelphia inventories indicate the existence of mahogany furniture in the 1690s and 1708 respectively. Mahogany from the West Indies was, in fact, used by

17 A Stuart chest in walnut and fruitwood reflects the growing opulence of life at the top in early 17th-century England. Intricate inlay of bone and mother-of-pearl is used with fine carving.

18 The colourful effect of Boulle—inlay of cut brass and tortoiseshell—is shown in this close-up of the top of a 19th-century card table in Louis XV style. Work by the master, André-Charles Boulle, commands astronomical prices.

19 Fine marquetry of garlands and shells on an early 19th-century Dutch walnut cabinet on chest. Marquetry is produced from intricate designs, cut from woods of contrasting colours and grains.

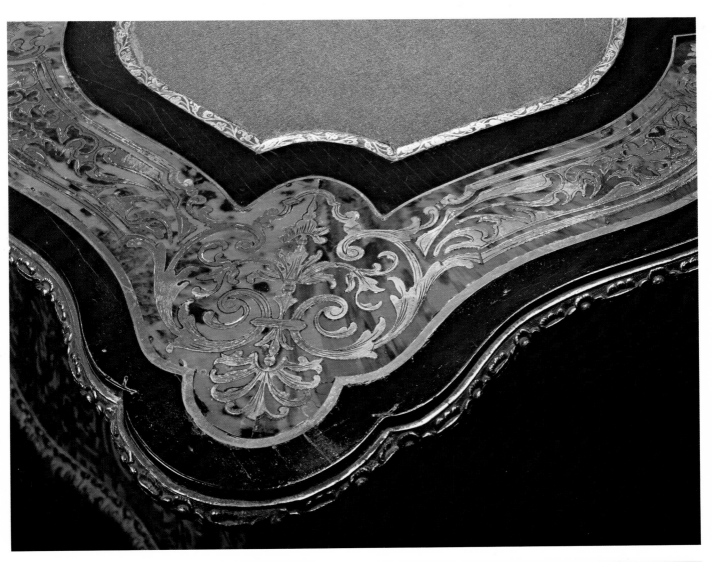

Sir Walter Raleigh to repair his ships in Elizabeth's day. It was not imported in quantity to England until about 1715, but some earlier shipments crossed the Atlantic and it is known that mahogany was occasionally made up into furniture in England in the latter half of the 17th century. Its colour varies from red-brown to golden, and it is tough enough for the delicate, lacy carving epitomised by Thomas Chippendale, master cabinet-maker, who gave his name to a whole genre of furniture on both sides of the Atlantic.

The son of a joiner and picture frame maker who had migrated from the provinces to London, Thomas Chippendale was born in 1718 and died in 1779. He relied solely on carving for ornament, rejecting all inlay. His chairs were masterpieces of fine proportion and symmetry, varying from the more solid earlier creations on cabriole legs to his straight-legged models, with delicate ribbon carving in the backs. Later still, his clients' tastes led him to the Gothic style with arches and tracery in chair backs. His designs embraced all forms of furniture and accessories from bureau bookcases to mirrors, overmantels and even tea caddies. He was a shameless adaptor of ideas – the ideas of the Dutch, the French, the Chinese and the Gothic Revivalists. Before his time, well designed furniture was for the wealthy and privileged.
25   Under his influence, good taste reached out to all classes.

In 1754 he published his first edition of *The Gentleman and Cabinet-Maker's Director* at £2 8s. and announced, indeed, that his designs were 'calculated to improve and refine the present taste and suited to the fancy and circumstances of persons in all degrees of life'. His book was for the 'Gentleman and the Cabinet-Maker' to 'assist the one in the choice, and the other in the execution of the designs'. It was in fact a style book, invaluable to furnituremakers remote from day to day contact with London fashions. It ran to three editions, the third being priced at a costly £3 13s. 6d. (In November 1971 a 1754 edition in good condition sold at auction for £525.) Circulation was wide. For instance, 15 copies of the first edition were bought in Yorkshire, half a dozen English Dukes subscribed, and merchants of Boston and Philadelphia sent for copies to instruct their furnituremakers.

Real Chippendale is scarce because the collecting vogue for his work started early, but his followers produced many good copies, and their ubiquitous
26   versions of his mahogany chair with squarish back and straight or cabriole legs are as near to Chippendale as most of us will ever get. Only experience will provide the know-how to distinguish between true and 'in-the-style-of' Chippendale. However a few points are useful to the collector. Chippendale had access to a mahogany of excellent quality, infinitely better than the inferior type which came later from Honduras. With such good and ample material at hand, he never stinted on his carving, so that his chair splats have a delicacy which

21 A slat-back rocker from New England of around 1750. Part of its description sounds like something from a menu: sausage-turned stiles capped with mushroom finials. Painted and grained to resemble walnut and bird's-eye maple, it realised $225 at auction in New York in 1973.

often escapes the work of the country maker. The proportion of space in relation to wood in a chair back was always finely balanced. Further, the master or those under his direct influence would chamfer the wood of splats from the back to give them a more fragile appearance, a nicety which might be overlooked by the country maker or those abroad who worked from a *Director* design shown in full face. An added complication was the nature of some of the drawings in his book. It is said that many were the work of Matthias Darly, who engraved the plates, and frankly some appear to be unworkable as furniture structures. One case in point is a pedestal desk which would simply break in the middle if made as drawn.

Much of Chippendale's later work was influenced by the French style known as Rococo, developed during the reign of Louis XV (1715–1774). Having said that, however, I must stress that he made no attempt to follow its worst excesses. After the masculine Baroque of Louis XIV, Rococo was a fantastic style of feminine elegance, but in its search for ornament at any price it later overstepped

29

22 Marquetry—a 'seating' of veneers arranged in patterns—decorates this 18th-century Dutch bureau of bombé, or swollen, style. Much in favour in Victorian England, Dutch marquetry is now the target of Italian and Spanish buyers.

23 Of typically English derivation is the bureau cabinet, seen here in a Queen Anne walnut example. The hinged fall front comes down to rest on pull-out supports, revealing an interior fitted with nests of shelves and small drawers.

24 North American Indian masks carved in gesso, a hardened composition, reveal transatlantic influence in the marble-topped side table from the reign of George I. The legs are the fashionable cabriole, ending in foliate scroll feet.

the bounds and indulged in meaningless trivia. A common motif, in addition to C-scrolls and shells, was rockwork, *rocaille*–hence Rococo. It was the age of the voluptuous boudoir rather than the grand salon, and in fact many of the huge galleries at Versailles were chopped up into smaller rooms during the reign of Louis XV and the earlier Regency under Philippe, Duke of Orleans. Straight lines were taboo; it was a time for the bombé, or swollen, look for commodes of drawers. Furniture followed the whims of the court, which itself followed the whims of such arbiters of taste as Madame de Pompadour and Madame du Barry. Appropriately in such an era of feminine finery and influence, the bureau plat or writing table illustrated is known as 'the table of Catherine II', having once belonged to the Russian Empress. It was removed from Rose Terrace, Grosse Pointe Farm, Michigan, in 1971 and sold in London by Christie's for Mrs Anna Thomson Dodge at £31,500.

In theory, French influence should have been supreme in American furniture of the late 18th century, as all things British were 'out'. Despite the War of Independence, however, Thomas Chippendale succeeded where George III, his ministers and generals failed. True, French Rococo carving showed in Philadelphia work, but after all this was a message propagated by Chippendale himself, as we have seen. His *Director* was the bond which tied the American furniture industry to London, and two editions of it were already available when Philadelphia craftsmen adopted the Chippendale style around 1760, fifteen years before the war. Attempting to date American furniture of this period by the various styles of the master is a hit-and-miss business. The Philadelphians had practically the whole Chippendale range from which to choose, and a cabinetmaker could work from a late design one year and revert to an earlier design a few years after. American craftsmen fell into

25 'In Chippendale taste' is a phrase we often meet. Here, it describes a George III mahogany wine table, with a pie crust top shaped like a silver salver.
26 A Chippendale style mahogany dining chair demonstrates the master's interlaced ribbon backs. Also characteristic are the finely carved 'knees' of the chair legs.

27 The artistry of the French at its highest: an important Louis XV marquetry table. Maker Jean-Pierre Latz insisted on fashioning the gilt-bronze corner mounts (ormolu) himself in contravention of the strict Guild laws in Paris which allotted certain tasks to certain groups of craftsmen.
28 The cabriole, or bandy, leg is shown in its full elegance in this fine George II side table. The top is inlaid with brass.

similar traps to those which met English country makers when translating the designs. Their chairs tended to be smaller, and the seat rails at the front were deeper, giving a board effect which marred the proportions of the design. Despite such variants, however, many captured the Chippendale spirit so successfully that it is difficult to say whether certain chairs are English or American.

One of Philadelphia's leading makers, who was accorded his true worth many years after his death, was Jonathan Gostelowe (c. 1744–1795). A craftsman and pillar of the church in Philadelphia, he broke off from cabinetmaking to serve as a major in the War. He is now acknowledged to be the author of several massive chests of drawers, the chests on chests, which had developed into the American highboy, rising to greater heights than any English tallboy chests. Another Philadelphian with revolutionary connections, who made highboys among many other types of furniture, was Benjamin Randolph, said to have fashioned the box desk on which the Declaration of Independence was drafted. **32**

It is from this time of American Chippendale, if not from its main theme, that a distinctive furniture arose in Newport, Rhode Island. It was a type not found in Europe, although some authorities say the seeds of the style were Dutch. The block front was usually applied to bureaux or slant-top desks and chests of drawers. **33** Carved in one piece, the blocking consisted of raised sections on the front of the furniture, each being separated by a concave section. A few block fronts from Rhode Island and Massachusetts, where they were sometimes made, occasionally turn up at sales in Britain,

Buroe Tables.

29 An example of 'impossible' Chippendale. This design from Thomas Chippendale's *Director*, shows a 'Buroe Table' which is supposed to be 4 ft 8 in. wide, and yet it is supported on bracket feet on the outside of the pedestals only. Furniture specialists declare that the weight would cause the table to sag or break in the middle.

30 C-scrolls in ormolu, a common decoration of Louis XV furniture, adorn this commode. Kingwood of contrasting grain—brought from South America and named in tribute to Louis—is used in combination with the marble slab top to achieve a somewhat restrained effect compared with many French pieces of this period.

31 A Chippendale walnut desk with gently undulating front of a style known as oxbow. It was made in Massachusetts between 1760 and 1780, an early example of American Chippendale.

32 A Chippendale carved mahogany side chair, dating from about 1770 and attributed to Benjamin Randolph of Philadelphia, demonstrating the 'board' look of the front seat rail, typical of many American Chippendale chairs, compared with the narrower rail of English chairs (see 26).

having been shipped across the Atlantic in the last two hundred years presumably for their curiosity value. When they appear, prices are high, and inevitably they find their way back to the American continent again.

The late 18th century presents difficulties in identifying the makers of many pieces of furniture. Descriptions abound with phrases such as 'Hepplewhite style', 'Sheraton taste', 'in the manner of', 'George III' and 'late 18th-century'. The period saw designs being propagated far and wide in a rash of furniture guides and drawing books more or less in the format of Chippendale's *Director*. Thomas Sheraton's *Cabinet-Maker and Upholsterer's Drawing Book* of 1791–1794 had an advance order for 782 copies. Several crossed the Atlantic, and its classical message was well received in

the emergent republic. A cabinetmaker in Russia with the incongruous name of Dillon subscribed to it (less surprising when we know that several British craftsmen were employed at the Imperial court). Peter Reid, oddly enough a 'Grocer and Tea Dealer of Whitehaven in Cumberland', was on the list. At the other side of the world, early settlers moving away from Australia's convict image fashioned Sheraton designs in local cedar wood.

In England the period is known by the names of the great designers Hepplewhite, Adam and Sheraton. In America it saw the beginning of the Federal period which was to last the first quarter of the 19th century. The French executed Louis XVI and, after the wasteful holocaust of the Reign of Terror, embraced the classical

33 This Massachusetts mahogany bureau from around 1770 has a block front. Although block fronts were made in Massachusetts, their true home is Newport, Rhode Island.

revival of the First Empire.

Excavations at the Roman cities of Pompeii and Herculaneum earlier in the century had stimulated design throughout Europe. Many London buildings bear the classical stamp, thanks to the work of architect Robert Adam (1728–1792), one of four talented sons of a Scottish architect: for instance the Adelphi, No. 20 Portman Square and the gateway to the Admiralty, and elsewhere great houses like Syon and Kenwood. More than an architect, however, Adam guided the furniture and interior decoration of his houses, giving them a lightness of form and an economy of classical line. Adam worked in close alliance with Chippendale on some projects including Harewood House in Yorkshire for which Chippendale designed the Chinese-style com-

mode discussed in the introductory chapter. Strangely, little if any Adam furniture has been discovered in America, but his hand is seen clearly in many Hepplewhite and Sheraton designs which made such a large impact there.

George Hepplewhite's origins are unknown. When he died in 1786 his widow carried on the business and two years later brought out his contribution to 18th-century do-it-yourself literature, *The Cabinet-Maker and Upholsterer's Guide*. Despite the late publication of his book, his designs had been around and had been executed for some time. Oval and circular card tables, unmistakably in Hepplewhite style, were advertised in the *Pennsylvania Packet* of 1785. The *Virginia Gazette* of 27th December 1787 offered furniture manufactured in Philadelphia, including circular and square card tables and commode chairs 'all inlaid'. Inlay was not used in Chippendale America, and again the reference is obviously to Hepplewhite's methods. His chairs are recognisable for their open backs of shield and heart shapes, their elegance of legs and their use of graceful curves. Bookcases, crowned by architectural pediments, often in swan's neck shape, were fronted in glass traced with ovals, rectangles and arches. Settees had elaborately turned legs, and his popular motif was the Prince of Wales' feathers.

Before turning to Thomas Sheraton, the last name in the triumvirate of 18th-century furniture designers (although these were but a fraction of the talented cabinetmakers who helped to make the period memorable), events in France warrant examination.

Louis XVI began his reign in 1774 and departed headless in 1793. During his time Rococo contortions calmed down considerably, although the feminine influence was still strong. Many of the writing and work tables and other smaller items of charm which were designed for Marie Antoinette are at Fontainebleau, in the Louvre, the Wallace Collection and the V & A. The boudoir look continued to dominate. Painted walls with a silk sheen finish, cupids and rose chains were the forerunners of wallpaper. Small and delicate furniture, often employing marquetry of rosewood, laburnum, holly and tulipwood, was made. It was still the day of the petite commode, a pretty item for madame's room. In furniture on the grander scale, the name of Jean-Henri Riesener stood high. With the title of *ébéniste* (cabinetmaker) to Marie Antoinette, he created sumptuous furniture, some of the finest ever made, in a climate of lush patronage. Sadly, the French Revolution of 1789 was followed by the Terror which saw the clearing out of noble homes, and much fine furniture was thrown to foreign dealers at a fraction of its true value. Rococo was dead; long live Classicism. Ideas of Rome and Greece were embraced with revolutionary fervour in the First Empire, and Egyptian influence spread after Napoleon's Nile cam-

34 The Prince of Wales' feathers, a favourite carving of George Hepplewhite, are a prominent feature of this shield-back armchair. The royal feather motif continued in America even long after the Revolution.

35 Classical influence is strong in this small mahogany occasional table designed by Robert Adam. It has gently fluted and tapering legs.

36 The boudoir look dominated the salons of France in the reigns of Louis XV and Louis XVI. Mirrors reflected the elegance of painted walls, and flowered carpets covered the floors. Rooms still had a feeling of space, however, uncluttered by too much furniture, as shown by this 19th-century retrospective painting by Victoriano Codina y Langlin. Note the centrally placed petite commode for m'lady's use.

37 Hepplewhite's famous shield-back chair. The interlaced back is carved with laurels, ribbons, husks and a fan rosette. The stuff-over seat is characteristic of the time, and legs are simple, square and tapering.

38 Elegance and utility mark the best of the designs of Thomas Sheraton who, despite his fame, lived and died in poverty. Both qualities are evident in this cheveret, a writing table with a detachable book trough which has a carrying handle. The wood is mahogany. Its price is in the £1,500 to £2,000 bracket.
39 A Sheraton mahogany sideboard has a cellarette at each side for the storage of wine. It has a gentle serpentine curve at the front, slender tapering legs on spade feet and narrow inlay, or crossbanding, of tulipwood.

paign of 1798. The new century dawned in a plethora of griffins, sphinxes, lion's heads, claw feet and ram's heads.

38 Thomas Sheraton (1751–1806) derived much from the styles of Louis XVI and, as we know, was influenced by Adam's interpretation of the classical line. He was a master of scale. His satinwood furniture designs of refined, rectilinear form are instantly recognisable. Yet there is no evidence that he ever made a piece of furniture for sale in his life. His story presents an enigma. Born poor at Stockton-on-Tees in Durham, he moved to London and lived in hardship all his life. One visitor calling on the family for tea describes how Mrs Sheraton had to drink out of the baby's mug as there were only two cups and saucers in the house – strange circumstances for a man whose repute was not entirely posthumous: it is known, for instance, that he designed an ingenious pair of library steps for George III. Perhaps he tried to do too much, for besides being a prolific author of furniture manuals and an art teacher he was a fervent and active Baptist preacher. His trade card read: 'T. Sheraton, No. 106 Wardour Street, Soho, teaches Perspective, Architecture and Ornaments, makes Designs for Cabinet-makers, and sells all kinds of Drawing Books etc.'

Treatises on furniture in his *Drawing Book* reflect his evangelical zeal and are written with an arrogance and a conviction that God was on his side. Professional etiquette caused him no qualms, and he lambasted other eminent cabinet designers with gusto. Of Chippendale's work he wrote airily: 'As for the designs themselves, they are wholly antiquated, and laid aside, though possessed of great merit according to the time in which they were executed.' Of Hepplewhite's furniture, he wrote: '. . . if we compare some of the designs, particularly the chairs, with the newest taste, we shall find that this work has already caught the decline, and perhaps, in a little time, will suddenly die in the disorder . . . they serve to show the taste of former times.' Strong words considering that they were written only two years after the publication of the second edition of Hepplewhite's *Guide*!

Sheraton's favourite wood was satinwood, of yellowish-brown colour from trees in the West and East Indies, shown off to its best effect when coupled with a carefully limited use of marquetry as preached from Wardour Street. Occasionally mahogany was used and sometimes tulip, apple and rosewood, the last being a Brazilian wood of varying degrees of colour which became very **61, 62** popular in the 19th century. Sheraton's *Drawing Book* gave detailed instructions, often running to great length on furniture which incorporated his ideas for secret drawers and sliding compartments and other moveable parts. Chairs had a fine rectangular look, usually without stretchers in England, although stretchers are a distinctive feature of American Sheraton chairs. Legs were finely tapered. Sideboards were of elegant proportions with slightly curved or serpentine fronts. Bureaux, bookcases, all manner of cabinets, sofas, knife boxes, clocks, tables, bedsteads, canterburies for sheet music, entire interiors – all were given the Sheraton treatment. Understandably from the man who preached in two dimensions, there is even a design for a pulpit. Besides his universal *Drawing Book*, he published *Designs for Furniture* and also the *Cabinet Dictionary*. Undaunted by his poverty-stricken lot, he ploughed on religiously with his last major work, *The Cabinet-Maker, Upholsterer and General Artist's Encyclopaedia*. He had reached the Cs when death overtook him in 1806.

Sheraton had a lasting influence well into the 19th century, no less in America than in his own country. In New York, Duncan Phyfe (1768–1854) stands out as a notable exponent of his tradition. The Baptist preacher supplied the basis for much of Phyfe's early work. This was to develop into a distinctive Phyfe style, making an important and colourful contribution to American furniture of the 19th century.

The 19th century
Collector's ground

On the eve of the great age of machinery and mass production of furniture, directions of influence between England, France and America become somewhat blurred. Communications were improving, ideas were exchanged with more rapidity and expansion was the keynote on both sides of the Atlantic. Terms such as Regency, Empire, Federal and Late Federal become inextricably mixed.

In England, the Regency period serves to take furniture well into the 1830s and, in fact, encompasses the last years of George III's reign when George, Prince of Wales, ruled as Regent (1811–1820) owing to his father's illness. He became George IV in 1820 and stayed on the throne for another ten years. Mild and unremarkable, William IV then ruled for seven years, a reign totally lacking in impact, until his niece, Victoria, took over for her marathon session in 1837.

English Regency furniture was usually veneered in mahogany, satinwood or rosewood, that richly marked favourite of 19th-century cabinetmakers. Among other finely figured woods which enjoyed popularity was the
69 amboyna wood of the West Indies. Zebra wood, beech
41 painted black and gold, and kingwood all made their contribution. It was a time of brass inlay for ornament, and marquetry was quite out of fashion. Egyptian lion's-
70 paw motifs and Grecian curves were strong in evidence. Chairs often had the classic sabre leg and were decorated
40 by newly revived, but restrained carving on top rails. Naturally, it was a time which saw much of the triple Prince of Wales' feathers, and in addition naval designs such as twisted cables, telescopes and dolphins were given their vogue by Trafalgar and other victories. Oddly, across the sea the royal feathers were still being used in Federal America, but there the eagle symbol of the new republic was appearing more frequently.

So much emphasis has been placed on the bizarre
42 examples of Regency furniture, which could run to massive proportions with sphinxes, animal legs and huge X-frames based on antiquity, that we can overlook the
68 simple elegance of a Regency day-bed with its curve-over end and delicate Chinoiserie decoration. The sofa typifies the leisurely essence of Regency times, and not only for the wealthy, it seems. In 1833, J. C. Loudon whose *Encyclopaedia of Cottage, Farmhouse and Villa Furniture* was a social as well as a furnishing document, wrote: 'A sofa is a piece of furniture which affords a great source of comfort to its possessor and therefore the cottager ought to have one as well as the rich man. Let him strive to obtain it, for no parlour is completely

furnished without one; and he will certainly succeed.' Whether the status of any cottager was improved by this means is not known, but certainly the fortunes of many a demi-mondaine have been advanced by the sofa or day-bed.

New types of furniture appeared. There was the sofa
4 table, which would have a rectangular top with flap at each end for extension, lyre supports and two drawers in the frieze. Ladies used it when writing or serving tea or coffee and sometimes perhaps a small meal. The
7 davenport, or small writing desk, came into its own and
1 heralded a hundred variations to come later in Victorian times. And, of course, there was the music canterbury which, we already know, had not escaped the attentions of Sheraton. Mirrors had become an everyday part of decoration in the drawing rooms of England and this period saw the development of the circular convex looking-glass in a gilt frame, as well as the tall cheval glass for full length viewing. Swing frame toilet mirrors,
1 which could show a squarish, mahogany look in Georgian England, assumed feminine curves and lacquered ornament. Historical romances helped feed the country's appetite for the Neo-Gothic, giving rise to architectural absurdities of furniture. In contrast to this extreme, however, examine a pair of cabinets from around 1815,
9 most attractively decorated in penwork style and, far from being grotesque, the exquisitely painted Gothic arches give the cabinets an air of fragile beauty.

In America, the aftermath of the republic's birth saw changing centres of gravity in the furniture industry. New York, Baltimore and trade-conscious Salem grew stronger at the expense of Philadelphia, Boston and Newport. Salem, for instance, was busy exporting furniture to the South and beyond. A secretary bookcase, owing much inspiration to Sheraton and bearing the label 'Nehemiah Adams, Cabinet-maker, Newbury Street (near the Common), Salem, Massachusetts', made its way to Cape Town. Thus America's furniture was no longer being produced solely for a local settler's market. Birch, satinwood and bird's-eye maple were being used for veneers, paint and gilt decoration, and where ormolu was too expensive stencilling was brought into play.

The most prolific and certainly the best-known name in American furnituremaking is, of course, that of Duncan Phyfe. Born near Inverness in Scotland in 1768, he came to Albany, New York, with his parents in his early teens. Later, with several years experience of furnituremaking in the Hepplewhite tradition, he moved to Partition Street, New York, in 1795 and there became

40 The simple elegance of Regency dining chairs. Light carving on the top rail is typical.

41 Beechwood has been japanned to simulate rosewood in these Regency dining chairs. Their sabre legs are one of the hallmarks of the era.

42 An English rosewood chiffonier–sideboard with two doors enclosing shelves–demonstrates the use of chimeras, or mythical beasts, common in

Regency days. This piece is in the manner of Thomas Hope (c. 1771–1831), an amateur furniture designer who worked in heavily classical style.

a devoted follower of Sheraton. Soon the Astor family were his clients and he worked in growing fame until the ripe age of 79, thereafter spending seven well fed years in retirement. Some say his name was originally the Scottish Fife, which he changed for a more popular French spelling in the new republic. Whatever the truth, he was not slow in seizing ideas from his British compatriots in his early and middle years. Today he is mainly remembered for the use of classical Greek styles, incorporating the lyre design for supports and chair splats, and animal legs and feet.

The age of elegance closed to a background of momentous social and industrial changes in the making. In Britain the machine age created a new middle class with tastes and outlook far removed from those of the Regency elite. Social patterns were set and were to last through the century. In 1880 Cassell's *Household Guide* declared:

A good housemaid will rise at six, and have her grates and rooms swept by seven . . . By nine o'clock breakfast ought to be cleared away . . . By eleven o'clock the upstairs work ought to be done . . . Washing up china and glass, dusting the drawing room, and other light labour of the kind may take till twelve or one o'clock, by which time the housemaid ought to be dressed for the day, fit to answer the door,

wait on the family and do needlework . . . At dusk, it is a housemaid's place to close all windows . . . Before going to bed she has to turn down all the beds of the family, replenish ewers and water bottles, empty slops and put everything in place . . . Considerate employers will dispense with a housemaid's attendance by ten o'clock, bearing in mind her morning duties . . .

The 'considerate employer' of Victorian days was recommended to pay the sum of £10 to £14 *a year* to his housemaid engaged on this prodigious 16-hour day. Thus the life style adopted by a striving and prosperous 19th-century middle class depended on a cheap and ready source of servant labour. The machine age, unlocking the secrets of mass production, had made available to a growing public some of the fruits hitherto enjoyed only by the very rich. No longer was it a case of craftsmen-made products being commissioned under wealthy patronage. Mr Chippendale and his successors had propagated the gospel far and wide. By the time young Victoria came to the throne in 1837 the industrial revolution was under way, and a merchant economy, reaping wealth from a vast Empire, was endowing the middle class with unprecedented spending power. It was a spending power all too often unallied with taste

44

or discrimination, resulting in lapses which have given Victorian design a bad name for so long. Ironically, many of these lapses in taste derived from Victorian attempts to emulate the best of the past. The word 'style' is symptomatic of the Victorian period of furniture manufacture – and the term 'manufacture' is used advisedly, because furnituremaking belonged more to industry than to art until the disciples of William Morris bestirred themselves in the last quarter of the century. The dominant machine having replaced the skill of the individual craftsman, it is hardly surprising that there was a dearth of designers of the calibre of the 18th century's golden age of furniture. And it is even less surprising that the new technology was harnessed to reproduce the styles of the past – Regency, Rococo,

Baroque, Elizabethan and the enigmatic 'modern English Gothic'. However, all cannot be bad in such an era of human endeavour, and Victorian furniture offers many good pickings for the modern collector. In variety alone, it makes for colourful study.

Several styles of furniture – all of fairly contemporary make, but representing widely different periods – might meet in a Victorian drawing room of England, or in its counterpart on the Continent. A 19th-century painting by Conrad Kiesel makes the point. Lavishly upholstered ladies sit on lavishly upholstered chairs. One chair is heavily tasselled and fringed, as is the patterned table-cloth. Another chair has a change of style in a leather back, slipping two centuries away from the contemporary scene. Patterned carpet vies with patterned wallpaper.

Globes, maps, books (for this seems to be a library corner) jostle with vases, a marble bust, drapery, a shell on a dolphin plinth. The effect is of unmitigated clutter, but what invitingly fertile ground it would be for the modern antiques hunter! Small wonder then that the housemaid had her time cut out in the Victorian household, with room after room similarly furnished.

Early Victorian days were designed for an indoor society. It was an era of draught-exclusion, of lighting the parlour lamps on a family esconced in upholstered comfort. Substantial mahogany and rosewood without veneer or marquetry were the basic woods of fashion. Although the dining table was a rectangle whose top extended, leaving a gap to be filled by a portable piece, it was the day of the round parlour table. Variations were made, sometimes round, sometimes oval, for use at breakfast or other non-formal meals, and these tables were usually on four heavy carved feet, supporting a thick central turned column. (Such a table sold at auction in London in 1971 for £60: the Victorian upsurge – coupled with inflation – accounted for an auction price of £150 for a similar rosewood example in late 1974.) The family sat in balloon-back chairs, which were more comfortable than their appearance suggested. Well stuffed upholstered seats completely covered the framework, and this upholstered look, disguising most of the structure, was applied to sofas as well as chairs. All manner of fabrics – velvets, silks, horsehair cloth dyed black – were used as well as leather. Upholstered backs and arms would be thickly padded and buttoned down. Much of the buttoning was very deep, and shallow buttoning can sometimes be the mark of a recently re-covered piece. 'We used to burn button-backs,' says a country auctioneer. 'Now they sell like hot cakes.'

The sofa, or day-bed, with one roll-over end and half back, was designed for one person when reclining. The

46

45 A fine product of the American furniture industry in late Georgian days was the chest on chest, here made in mahogany.

46 After a century of spacious aristocratic salons came the overfurnished bourgeois parlours of the 19th century. In contrast to the surroundings of the Louis ladies (see 36) is this 19th-century painting (*Story Time*) by Conrad Kiesel of a contemporary scene. Heavy patterned wallpaper, flowered tablecloth, deeply upholstered chair and a forest of bric-à-brac fill the room.

47 The Victorian home needed tables for all purposes. This is an oval walnut breakfast table with typical heavily decorative central column and carved feet.

48 The balloon-back chair, symbol of the Victorian era, with its dark mahogany look and stuff-over seat.

49 Another example of the balloon-back shape, this time in walnut, with open arms.

50 The 19th-century furniture industry in Europe and America often turned to the styles of the past. This German ebonised and porcelain cabinet borrows heavily from the Baroque age of the previous century.

51 Ormolu decoration in close focus. These splendidly moulded and gilded bronze mounts decorate much French furniture. They served both as decoration and as protection of corners and edges. Here it is employed on a 19th-century jardinière table in the style of Louis XV and is combined with walnut marquetry for effect.

52 Deep buttoning was a feature of many Victorian settees of fancy shape and carved frames.

53 An English Victorian cabinet in walnut embodies corner shelves for displaying a china collection.

54 The 19th century was a period of 'styles' and reproductions, such as this display cabinet in the Louis XV taste.

settee was usually a two- or three-seater of more elaborate construction. The ottoman entered the scene for formal occasions, being a long low bench heavily padded and possibly fringed and tasselled. Then there was the double armchair: two chairs fixed together, facing opposite directions, to enable two to have a tête-à-tête, yet hardly a discreet one as by its very nature this oddity had to stand in the centre of a room.

50

53 Cabinets and sideboards erupted in elaborate carving. Shelves proliferated to enable the Victorian housewife to indulge her fancy for displaying bric-à-brac. Corner shelves, enclosed by glass doors, appeared on otherwise simple cupboards to house the china and ornaments. There grew a forest of whatnots, three-tiered stands to hold all the mass of treasured Victoriana which beggared classification: decorated shells, pot lids, Staffordshire castles, fairings, pastille burners.

Chests of drawers retained their bow fronts from Regency times and round wooden knob handles were common. By the late 1850s the dressing table with built in drawers and mirror was appearing, signalling the demise of the elegant toilet mirror of earlier years. The use of cosmetics was frowned upon, so nests of tiny toilet drawers were out. For a generation obsessed with cleanliness, however, washstands were in. Many are still around from Victorian and Edwardian homes and are attractive and reasonably inexpensive items of furniture, with their clean pine and oak look, inlaid tiles and provision for one or two sets of jug, bowl and soap dish, with chamber pot en suite.

In the latter half of the 19th century the craze for

55 A pair of early 18th-century walnut
elbow chairs with a type of arm known as a
shepherd's crook. Chair furniture had taken
a major step forward with the upholstered
seat.

56 'Wierdies' from an age which demanded
elaboration and overdecoration: a pair of
Victorian rosewood chairs of strange design
in their splayed backs.

57 Chinese influence, stemming from
Netherlands trade with the East, showed in
much Dutch furniture. These side chairs of
the mid 18th century are decorated in
lacquer Chinoiserie designs.

54

56

variety produced a rash of reproduction Sheraton,
Chippendale and earlier styles. Louis XV and XVI,
Elizabethan, Renaissance, 'early English' and Gothic
flavours were essayed with varying degrees of success.
Machine age technology was often responsible for
excellent interpretations of bygone designs. On the
other hand, good design and comfort would sometimes
be thrust aside to satisfy the demand for the 'unusual'.

There was heavy flirtation with satinwood, tulipwood
and other veneers. Where only a cheaper wood could
be afforded it was stained to resemble satinwood.
Furniture tended to be lighter as the century matured.
Design was helped by ideas and materials brought back
from an Empire on which the sun never set. Thus we
had cane and bamboo. Later bentwood was used to
effect. Simple bentwood chairs with pierced plywood
seats were made in legion, the forerunners of those to be
found in smart 'design conscious' stores of today. The

use of cane in the rounded backs of high chairs afforded
a small degree of comfort to the Victorian baby. A year
or two older, however, and he was forced on to the
dreaded Astley Cooper, named after an eminent surgeon
whose chair pre-dated Victoria's accession but nevertheless had a long life in a society imbued with ideas of
correction. The chair was long and straight backed and
had double sets of stretchers at convenient juvenile foot
height. The back is composed of hard spindles beneath
a horizontal slat. J. C. Loudon's *Encyclopaedia* of 1833
describes the chair as 'recommended with a view of
preventing children from acquiring a habit of leaning
forward or stooping; the upright position of the back
affording support when the child is placed at table, and
eating, which a sloping backed chair does not. It is
proper to observe that some medical men do not approve
of these chairs.' Some of these relics turn up from time
to time and are prized for their curiosity value. Their

58 A 19th-century English cane-back high chair, which has a spring seat to allow the baby to bounce up and down. The wood is mahogany.

59 The organic, plant line showed strongly in Art Nouveau furniture at the end of the 19th century. Popularity of Art Nouveau in the early 1970s has meant consequent steep rises in saleroom prices for articles such as this mahogany secrétaire cabinet.

60 Papier-mâché furniture was an English Victorian innovation, often painted and highly varnished as in this chair. It was as solid as many woods.

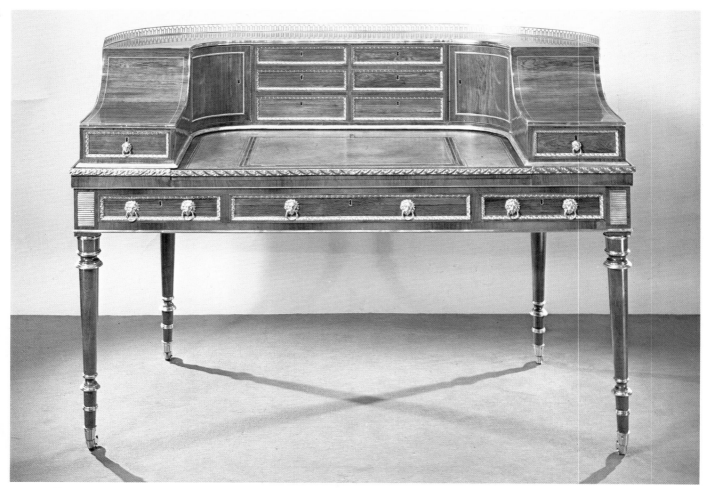

61, 62 A fine rosewood Carlton House table of around 1810, and the item as it appears in Sheraton's *Drawing Book*. The table is so called probably because an early example was made for the great house in London. There is controversy over whether the original design for such a table was Sheraton's; certainly the hollow flaps over the inkwells at each side are his inspiration.

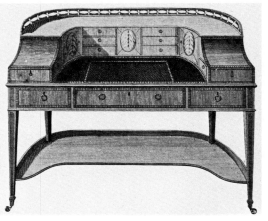

62

63 The bureau plat, or writing table, was usually designed for the man, in contrast to the feminine bonheur du jour (see 11). This Louis XV bureau plat, with oak carcase and kingwood veneer, was, however, the property of Empress Catherine II of Russia. In the 20th century it has graced the Mid West home of a wealthy American lady.
64 A superb product of French furniture design which came into general use about 1760 is the secrétaire à abattant, or fall front secrétaire. When lowered for use as a writing surface, the fall front is balanced by counterweights inside the cabinet. The doors below enclose a set of drawers. The material is tulipwood, from a Brazilian tree which bears tulip-shaped flowers.

65 An oak chair with rush seat from around 1910 demonstrates some of the best design attributes of Art Nouveau. It was made by Heal & Sons of London, and its graceful, vertical lines are similar to those found in furniture of the Shaker religious sect in America.

66 A beautifully made walnut settee in the Egyptian taste designed by Christopher Dresser. The back moves on a brass rod to face either way. It dates from 1870 to 1880 and is a forerunner of Art Deco.

place is more in a chamber of horrors than a furniture collection, as is the Victorian child's restraining chair, which is a wooden seat, walled in by wooden panels at child-proof height and enclosed by a solid gate which locks on the outside. I found one in a country antique shop, its seat mildewed by generations of damp and the interior of the gate scuffed and splintered by half a century of frustrated infantile kicking. Surely the saddest of antiques. I let it pass, though at £5 it was a bargain for any collector of oddities.

Cast iron came in, not only for hall and garden furniture, but combined with brass tubing for beds.

For sheer ingenuity the Victorians deserve honours in their use of papier-mâché. Machine processes made possible the manufacture of sophisticated pieces of furniture from paper which had been pulped and bound with a resinous substance. Not only trays and boxes, but tip-up tables, chairs and even sideboards were produced. When moulded and then lacquered, painted in bright colours or ornamented with gilt and mother-of-pearl, this furniture was as substantial as any of wood.

Inevitably mass production produced an artistic reaction, and the 1880s saw the growth of the Arts and Crafts Movement, stemming out of the teachings of, among others, William Morris, artist, designer and poet. The organic line, embodied in the swirling plant motif, was

60

the essence of the style which developed into Art Nouveau (a name taken from the title of a store opened in Paris in 1895 by an exponent of the new art form). Controversy raged – and still continues – around Art Nouveau. A French critic wrote in 1895: 'All this seems to have the air of a vicious Englishman, the Jewess addicted to morphine, the Belgian trickster, or a salad of these poisons.' Notwithstanding the Frenchman's xenophobia and anti-semitism, his passions were merely an echo of feelings elsewhere. At the turn of the century a consignment of furniture designed by the talented Louis Majorelle, of Nancy, was shipped from Paris to the South Kensington Museum (now the V & A). The

intention was to display the pieces in their full-blooded interpretation of the organic line for the benefit of students. Unfortunately critics declared that the designs were 'corrupting' and kicked up such a fuss that the exhibits were withdrawn and they languished in the cellars for over half a century. Only recently have the cabinets and chairs of Majorelle been given their right-ful recognition as superb examples of Art Nouveau furniture, and they are displayed at the Bethnal Green Museum in the East End of London.

And yet Art Nouveau was not preaching a wholly revolutionary message to the 19th-century world of capital and commerce. Indeed, its most ardent exponents

68 Regency leisure is epitomised in this day-bed, painted to resemble rosewood with Chinoiserie decoration.

69 Richly coloured amboyna wood from the West Indies is set off to fine effect in this centre table, with gilt decoration, of about 1825.

70 The classical lion's-paw feet of Regency days, seen here in one of a pair of cabinets veneered in burr yew and mahogany.

71 Australian piece—a cedar, swing-top card table, of about 1815. Note the massive moulded centre column and fluted bun feet.

argued that machine mass production should be harnessed to craftsmanship to make examples of the new art available to all. They demanded simply that quality of design and manufacture should be the hallmark of value rather than rarity or costliness of raw materials. In its development Art Nouveau borrowed from many themes. One was the Japanese, whose impact on furniture and wares had begun to be felt after Commodore Perry opened Japan to the West in 1859. There was also the Medieval or Gothic, a tide which had ebbed and flowed through furniture design for several centuries. The Roman, the Greek and the Egyptian fed the new art

form. And even before the end of the century Art Nouveau showed signs of developing a divergent direction from the organic, into the field of functionalism and severe cubism.

In America the 19th-century progress towards functionalism was made independently and by a small school of furniture designers motivated by quite different beliefs. Significantly, it was another revolt against commercialism, ostentation and extravagance, but with its roots deep in religion. The Shakers were a sect so called because of the contortions which form part of their ceremonial. Originally from England, the Shaking

66

72 A universal piece of furniture of the 19th century was the work table, with fabric pouch to hold sewing materials. This is a New South Wales cedar example of 1835.

Quakers settled in New York and later trekked to Ohio, Kentucky and Indiana. Never being more than a few thousand-strong, they nevertheless numbered among their people many craftsmen who produced a simple, clean and sturdy furniture of lasting repute. Eschewing all embellishments such as carving and inlay from principles of religious asceticism, their cupboards, boxes, chairs and tables pre-dated functionalism in Europe. Today the sect is moribund, and Shaker furniture is much sought by collectors.

Elsewhere on the American scene the religion of the dollar flourished in the 19th-century climate of expansion westward. Lambert Hitchcock, of Connecticut, who worked between 1820 and 1843, mass-produced chairs and settees in huge quantities. They are often classified as Federal and have a country charm allied to delicate paint and stencilwork decoration. Parts were machine-made, and the Hitchcock chair, with its turned legs and cross pieces, came from the same pattern for several decades. Fake-spotters should acquaint themselves with his work in museums, and with his signature, for he signed his chairs.

In America, as in Europe, a newly enriched society looked to the glories of the past for inspiration. The French Empire line, with its roots in Egypt, became known as the Late Federal. Gothic was followed by Neo-Rococo, Renaissance vied with the times of the three great Louis kings. The oriental style was strong in the 1870s and 1880s, but whereas in England it formed a mainstream of influence in Art Nouveau, furniture of the Arts and Crafts Movement was little made in the States. Ironically, it had been an American, James McNeill Whistler, who fired the English school with his passion for all things oriental, and he is remembered as a leading contributory spirit in English Arts and Crafts. The American will occasionally come across this 'Japanisation' of the late 19th century in bamboo furniture, usually made as bedroom suites.

Settler expansion in South Africa and Australia was leaving in its wake a society with growing resources and awareness of gracious living. The Dutch kas or **6** cupboard, which showed up in New York and New Jersey, made an early appearance in the Cape. The better-off Boer homesteads might also boast pieces of Cape Dutch marquetry furniture, derived from the home products, but fashioned in yellow wood and stinkwood, a hard, almost black, material which I am assured has no smell despite its unfortunate name. To Britain in the 19th century came much marquetry from **22** the Netherlands, and London is today the main hunting ground for Italian and Spanish dealers wishing to satisfy the demand in their own countries. Holland has little Dutch marquetry available. Such is the topsy-turvy nature of furniture-dealing economics. It is hardly surprising, therefore, with prices doubling in twelve months on the London market, that the dealers are combing South Africa for Cape Dutch marquetry.

Some of the early settlers in Australia took with them furniture from which copies were made on the spot. Much of this imported furniture was from the English provinces, and so already one step away from the influence of established London cabinetmakers. In translation in the new colonies it inevitably moved further away, thus accounting for a primitive look in **67, 71,** some early Australian pieces. The settler-cabinetmaker **72, 100** had only his local woods from which to work. In New South Wales he turned to cedar, in Tasmania Huon pine and cedar imported from New South Wales. However, isolation helped Australia to escape from much of the mid 19th-century blight of heaviness and over-ornamentation, and some of the colonial styles are unpretentiously elegant. Oddities there are, such as a Gothic monstrosity of a rosewood armchair, upholstered in kangaroo fur for Governor Macquarie. On the whole, however, good 19th-century furniture made in Australia earns itself the reputation which commands high prices today in the salerooms of Sydney and Melbourne.

Chairs

Ask any cabinet-maker, and he will tell you at once that his customers prefer the ornamented chair, and care nothing about the unity, or the want of unity, of style. Their great object is to get a display of rich workmanship, at as cheap a rate as possible. Our readers, we are sure, will agree with us that this taste on the part of the purchaser is of a vulgar and grovelling kind, and ought to be corrected.

J. C. Loudon
Encyclopaedia of Cottage, Farmhouse and Villa Architecture and Furniture, 1833.

One hundred years before J. C. Loudon was lecturing the British public on taste, a newspaper cutting of 1730 advertised an establishment which sounds more like a pub than a furniture shop—'At the Three Cover'd Chairs and Walnut-tree in St Paul's Churchyard . . .' There, John Brown sold 'all sorts of Windsor Garden Chairs, of all sizes, painted green or in the wood'. Not much more is known about this London chairmaker. His advertisement, however, is one of the earliest printed references to the Windsor chair, that universal, much varied and popular piece of seat furniture.

The Windsor chair is probably the most available, and therefore the most collectable item of old furniture on both sides of the Atlantic. George II bought one for £4, 'a very neat mahogany Windsor chair', Thomas Jefferson ordered a large set in black and gold, and Benjamin Franklin had two dozen in white. They came into use in England by the late 17th century, but were certainly widespread by the early 18th, and have lasted and are made until this day. Their connection with the town of Windsor is tenuous, to say the least. Possibly the Thames-side town was a useful distributing point for London, but the home of the true Windsor was in the beechwoods around High Wycombe, some 13 miles away from Windsor. There, ample supplies of beech were used for the spindles in the backs, for the legs, turned or cabriole, and for the stretchers. Traditionally, elm formed the seat which was carved into a saddle shape and is surprisingly comfortable despite its solidity.

As the chair's popularity widened, it was made in several variations for the wealthier homes as well as for cottages and gardens. In the better chairs yew—the wood from which the famous English longbow was fashioned— replaced beech or ash. Willow, mahogany and walnut have all been employed. Beech, incidentally, being soft is susceptible to worm, and any beechwood furniture should be thoroughly checked for the telltale holes.

The most common form of Windsor found in antique

73 The ubiquitous Windsor chair of yew and elm, seen here in a group of six all of which sport the crinoline stretcher uniting the legs.

74 Cabriole legs and turned legs, crinoline or cowhorn stretchers, pierced splats and wheelback – varying characteristics of the Windsor can be seen in these two English examples. Both are of the 18th century.

shops today is the hoop-back, a style which tends to place it after the middle of the 18th century. Earlier, the English Windsor was the comb-back, in which the upright spindles of the back were united at the top by a horizontal crosspiece, sometimes lightly decorated with carving. To add to the collector's difficulties in dating, however, this style was often followed on both sides of the Atlantic much later than 1750. Splats varied from the simple pierced types to those embodying a wheel design, the hallmark of the wheel-back. In practically all the armchair variety there is a horizontal rail, at mid back level, which curves round and is prolonged to form the arms, themselves supported by short spindles which could be simple dowels, heavily turned or carved to suit the maker's inclinations or the customer's pocket.

Harmonious curves went into making the stretchers, one of the most attractive types being the cowhorn, sometimes called 'crinoline' in English auction catalogues.

Windsors, it seems, met with the approval of the acidic J. C. Loudon who called them the best kitchen chairs in general use. His *Encyclopaedia* gives some of the chemistry secrets of the chairmaker: 'These chairs are sometimes painted, but more frequently stained in diluted sulphuric acid and logwood; or by repeated washing them over with alum water, which has some tartar in it; they should afterwards be washed over several times with an extract of Brazil wood. The colour given will be a sort of red, not unlike that of mahogany; and, by afterwards oiling the chair and rubbing it well, and for a long time, with woollen cloths, the veins and

74

75 Variety was the essence of American Windsors. These are from a set of eight made in Rhode Island between 1770 and 1780. They have braced hoop backs, seats of interesting shape and baluster turned legs and stretchers. The set realised a staggering $6,000 at a New York auction in 1973.

shading of the elm will be rendered conspicuous. Quicklime slacked in urine, and laid on the wood while hot, will also stain it of a red colour; and this is said to be the general practice with the Windsor chair manufacturers in the neighbourhood of London.'

A fascinating industry of Windsor chair making has lasted over the centuries in the beechwoods of the Chiltern Hills, and an entire chapter would be needed to do justice to its intricacies. However, a brief description of its function might interest the collector. Basically three roles were played by the Windsor chair craftsmen. There was first a bodger, an old English term for the turner who would work in the woods making the spindles, legs and stretchers, which were then sent to the town. There, the bottomer fashioned the saddle seats and the remaining parts of the chair. Finally it was the turn of the framer to assemble all the finished pieces.

What price do you pay for Windsor? The question is not easy to answer because of the enormous variations in style and quality. You may be lucky to find a battered, but eminently restorable, example for a few pounds. By early 1976, good quality late 18th-century elm and

yew armchairs were going in the London salerooms at prices from £80 to £150 each. At the top end of the scale, however, a writing-arm Windsor (embodying a flat writing surface on the right) sold in the United States at auction for $3,200. The writing-arm is peculiarly American, and on that side of the Atlantic much ingenuity was employed in variations of the Windsor. 75 Rockers are probably more common in America, although they appear also in English shops from time to time. A country auction in Britain recently saw a delightful pair, a full-size rocker with pierced splats and turned 76 spindles, accompanied by a child's rocker, with simple spindle uprights.

Earlier this book discussed the resurgence of oak, and before leaving the subject of country-inspired seat furniture, it is appropriate to look at a 17th-century oak stool of a type made on both sides of the Atlantic. 9, 78 Honest and solid, this furniture was made for seating people at the long table. It was not until around 1650 that the English stool was given an upward projection at the back to form a back-stool. Scuff marks on the stretcher, as we know, are often a sign of age, having

76 Two English rocker Windsors of the 19th century, the child's chair echoing the simple clean style of fullsize stick-backs.
77 Collapsible campaign chairs in mahogany, dating from George III's time. The carved seats lift upwards and the frames fold in concertina fashion. They are highly desirable items for collectors. These came in a set of six and were sold at auction for £399 in 1973.
78 A 17th-century style oak joined stool is typical of many 'coffin' stools, used as stands for coffins in English country churches.

been made by the feet of countless sitters. A further test is to turn the stool upside down for signs of wear on the under side as these low stools, when not in use, were stacked on the stretchers of the great table. Such a stool is often called a coffin stool from the practice of placing coffins on a pair in church. As a pair, the value advances disproportionately, but a word of warning here. Beware of two such stools whose resemblance to each other is too near. The craftsman of old practically never turned out two absolutely identical stools or chairs—and that goes also for the great makers of the 18th century, such as Chippendale or Hepplewhite. Chairs which match too closely in sets often mean a later reproduction in times when the machine had brought a finer degree of exactitude into the science of furnituremaking.

English oak stools can often run into three figures (the one illustrated made £270 in 1973, compared with the £10 paid for a similar stool at a Manchester auction in 1902). With diligence and luck, however, the collector can still find them in a neglected corner of a village antique shop. Their sheer strength and solidity of workmanship have stood the test of time, and there are still a fair number around. I have come across them in country churches, where sadly they have not always been cared for as they should. Years of placing porous flowers vases on them have ruined the tops of these splendid old stools.

Jacobean oak has a 'bloom' which it is almost impossible for the forger to copy. Only experience, however, will enable the collector to recognise this appearance. The look comes from the processes to which the wood was subjected, namely an application of varnish mixed with oil, which sank into the wood and was not merely a surface preservative as used in the 19th century. A similar treatment was given sometimes to early 18th-century beech to give it an 'oak' look. The modern faker will try to simulate the old 'bloom' by discolouring new oak with ammonia, following up with preparations which include the use of beeswax. One safeguard against this practice is to inspect the under edges of the wood, with their telltale 'new' look. Above all, make a friend of a trusted dealer. There are many in the trade, and their reputation and livelihood depend on good customers coming back to buy more.

Alongside the transition from oak to walnut and to mahogany, we have seen the development of styles such as the turned spiral, the cabriole, the straight tapering legs and many more. Perhaps the greatest revolution in chairmaking, however, was the introduction of upholstery. In Elizabeth I's reign chairs for the well-off had loose cushions, and upholstery was almost unknown. Although padded backs and seats were known by the reign of Charles I, the style of loose-cushioned chairs, often embodying cane, was still current across the length and breadth of Europe for most of the 17th century and

well into the 18th. Again, on the dawning of the 19th century, cane was used in collapsible campaign chairs, designed to bring a little comfort into the life of the officer out in the field. Campaign chairs appeal to many collectors because of their variety of style and uses. A popular type is the leather seated and backed chair with X-frame supports. Naturally, such a chair with eminent provenance—made, for instance, at the orders of Napoleon or Wellington—commands a high figure, but others need not be too expensive. Their absence of decoration places them in an accessible bracket for most

76

78

79 The famous Martha Washington or lolling chair, in mahogany and dating from the Federal period in America. The curved back and upholstered seat made it very comfortable.

80 These Queen Anne maple, rush-seat side chairs were made in Massachusetts between 1720 and 1740. That American styles trailed those in Europe is shown by the description 'Queen Anne'. The monarch had been dead for years when these chairs were made.

81 Rosewood and the balloon back, two common features of English Victorian dining chairs, are employed in this example.

77

99

middle-of-the-road collectors. Christie's of London in 1974 sold a mahogany set of six for £399, a reasonable figure for soundly made relics of George III's days.

Upholstery had reached accomplished levels by Hepplewhite's time, and a lot was seen of the stuff-over seat, fully covering the woodwork, which was to be a great favourite of the Victorians. Architect and designer Robert Adam reached new heights of elegance in his upholstered chairs, which made use of slender, decorated legs.

In America as in England changes in styles were more apparent in chairs than in other types of furniture. Maple was used to attractive effect, allowing intricate

turning, and when combined with rush seats the wood gave a distinctive American appearance to the high backed chair in mid 18th-century Massachusetts. The American collector has a rich field of chairs open to him, many of which reflect his national heritage. Some of them have been dealt with in earlier chapters, and the number of local variations down the eastern seaboard and further inland would need a huge volume for adequate study. Federal New England produced one particular late style which, for visual simplicity, put to shame some of the over-upholstered and ornate chairs of Victorian Britain. It was the lolling chair, known as the Martha Washington. There are many Martha

Washingtons about, though they have already found their place in the salerooms of Sotheby Parke Bernet and other grand auction rooms. In design they foreshadow chairs of the 1930s, with their tall upholstered backs, upholstered seats and open arms. Front legs are sometimes turned, others having a gentle sabre curve.

By this time the 19th century was ushering in the Victorian age in England, and chair design rested to a large extent on the triple beliefs of rosewood, balloon-back and stuff-over seat. Patently, in the various trends towards reproduction of the latter part of the century, old styles of former centuries were to express themselves. But as I seldom meet a collector who will admit that his

speciality is amassing *reproduction* furniture, the true products of Victorian England have more right to be discussed in this book.

Arms are absent on many Victorian easy chairs simply because the woman's skirt was becoming extremely voluminous. Seated on a low, upholstered chair which was thickly padded and buttoned down at the back, she could relax in comfort and display to advantage her fine dress. Similarly, space was the essence of design in the Victorian settee, a two-seater conversation piece, this, and not to be confused with the sofa meant for one person. A wooden framed back, deeply buttoned and representing human embracing arms, was a feature of

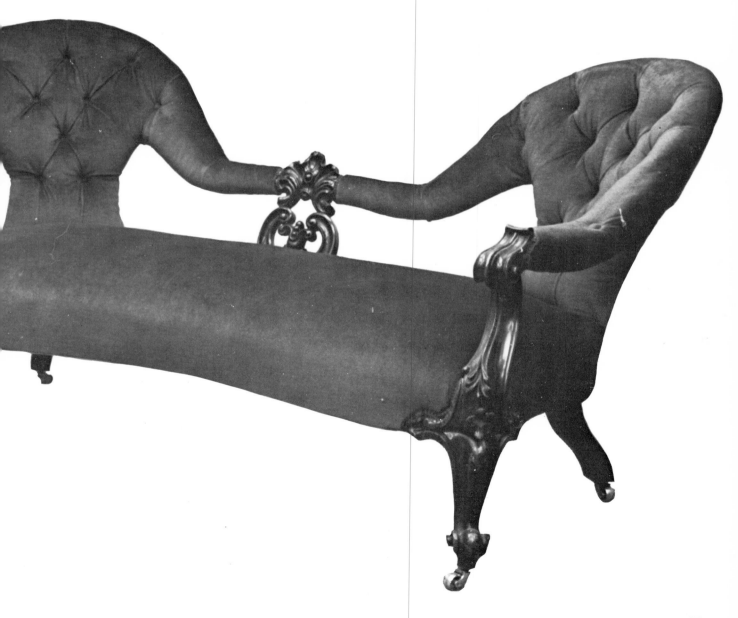

83 A strange 19th-century invention in Britain and the United States was this conversation settee, a form of public room furniture which made its way into the middle class home.

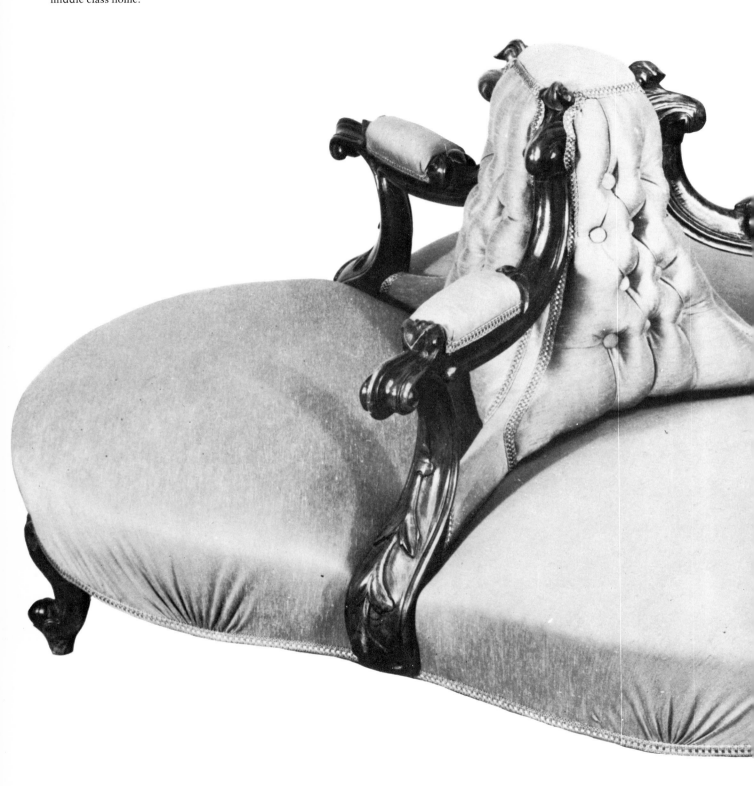

84 Made in their thousands were these Victorian sofas, intended for one person when relaxing. Solid, attractive pieces of living room furniture, they are reasonably inexpensive for the presentday collector. A widespread practice was the covering of all structural framework by the upholstery.

some of these settees sought by the bourgeois ladies of fashion. It was the era of great exhibitions in crystal palaces—New York, Philadelphia, Paris, London, hardly a major city of the Western world missed having such a show—and thus a distinctive type of 'public room' furniture developed, with fashion demanding its adoption in the home as well. This was the conversation settee, sometimes appearing as the double armchair. Others would take the form of three seats with their backs to a central, upholstered pillar, hybrid pieces of furniture as popular in America as in England. 82 83

As no other piece of furniture, however, the Victorian sofa with its roll-over end, is representative of the time. Availability being one of the greatest spurs to collectors, this item in its buttoned upholstery of velvet or similar material is a popular and cheap item in many an antique store on both sides of the Atlantic. Nevertheless, prices have risen, and an example which would have cost £40 at the beginning of the 1970s has been pushed up into the £100 bracket. Much depends on the condition of the upholstery, and if it is in poor order do remember that to have such a sofa re-upholstered can add another 50 per cent to the original cost. 84

Tables

A solid chunk of timber resting on trestles represented the earliest table. It was found in the great halls of the Middle Ages, and when not needed for dining it was dismantled and stored on one side. Refinements came slowly, but by the 17th century life around the stately home was demanding more than just a board at eating times. As casual entertaining became more customary, occasional tables with hinged folding tops appeared, often with turned column legs and a little carved decoration in the oak. Like all early oak, these once-neglected items of Stuart furniture have now taken off into the dizzy price climb.

From these rough and ready tables to the exquisite occasional tables with which the rich French furnished their salons in the next century is an enormous step. In the pampered atmosphere of the French court, the talented ébénistes, or cabinetmakers, were encouraged to fashion the finest furniture ever made by man. Such a piece is a Louis XV marquetry work table by Jean-Pierre Latz of Paris (c. 1691–1754). Just over 14 inches wide at the top, it stands on cabriole legs of such gentle curves and lightness that it appears to be living. Fine ormolu frames the kingwood marquetry. The interior is fitted with three working compartments and a drawer for writing materials. With all this excellence it is no surprise that its auction price level stands around £18,000. The stages which took tablemaking to this level were evolutionary and stemmed, as in all furniture design, from social changes. In England refinements came on apace after the monarchy was restored with Charles II in 1660. The familiar gate-leg table was now established and was to be a feature of English and

85

85 This half-round folding table by an English 17th-century maker has a hinged top. It is, of course, in oak, the universal wood of the time.

86 A card player with a feel for the exotic ordered this 18th-century card and tea table, lacquered in flowers and Chinese scenes.

American furnishing for several centuries. In America it later went through some interesting adaptations, acquiring the traditional American 'butterfly wings' of solid wood on the gates. Drawers were added to these tables before the end of the 17th century, and stretchers curved to meet in a finial, or decorative vertical feature, under the centre of the tables.

Interior design went hand in hand with furniture developments. Thus arose the pier table, gilded and with marble top, which was meant to be attached to the wall or pier between two windows and form with them and possibly a mirror, or pier glass, a composite unit of design. They were massive, ornately decorated pieces and, as few collectors are likely to seek them unless their home environment is on the grandest of scales, they can be left to one side in this survey of tables.

It is the field of the smaller, moveable tables which affords the collector the widest scope. Card playing, which had resulted in the first plain walnut card tables by 1690, became an English fever by the days of Queen Anne and the Georges. The craze took time to become established in America, but nevertheless the emergent nation was to produce its own quota of individually styled card tables. The first specially designed tables had folding rectangular tops with circular depressions in the corners to hold candles, and they also incorporated a shallow dish for the money. Through the 18th and 19th centuries the legs followed the currently popular form, whether cabriole or straight. Although the moral conscience of Victorian Britain frowned on gambling, card tables were a main stream of furniture until well into the 20th century, and on account of their variety several are illustrated here. The collector may go for a relatively inexpensive late 19th-century copy of a Queen Anne card table, or move to the other end of the scale, spending a small fortune on a masterpiece of marquetry. Such a piece is a fine and rare Russian marquetry card table dating from the last quarter of the 18th century, once in the Russian Imperial collection at the Hermitage in St Petersburg (Leningrad) and sold in 1973 from the estate of the late Sydney J. Lamon, of New York City. At auction in London it realised £11,550. A striking feature of this table is its top inlaid with a marquetry of different woods depicting music, instruments, scrolls and flowers. The woods (burr maple, tulip and rosewood) and the type of marquetry suggest that the table is of Russian origin, but the characteristic English form of the table probably owes something to the prevailing influence of English and Scottish artists working at the court of Catherine II.

The breakfast table of the 18th and early 19th centuries is a smallish (about 4 feet wide) circular table, standing on three or four splayed supports. It was meant for one or two persons and would be on castors to enable it to be pushed aside when not in use. Versions come with two small flaps, opening to provide a square top.

There were tables for tea and tip-up tables for reading, the latter standing on a tripod or on four legs with turned central column. In England and in the Philadelphia area there developed a table, variously described as a tea table or as a candle or lamp stand. It had a swivel top, quite small, sometimes resting on a 'birdcage' arrangement, and the edge of the top might have a waved gallery or a 'pie crust' border, similar to that on contemporary silver salvers.

Thomas Sheraton's designs covered the whole range of tables with many examples of the master-designer's celebrated inventiveness. A remarkable item in his *Drawing Book* shows the library table, which was basically a top laid over two drawer pedestals. Drawers on either side conceal reading stands which may be raised like easels. The overall effect, judging from the drawing, is somewhat graceless and surprising for a man who designed so much in elegance. He was more at home when designing the Pembroke table, the delicate occasional furniture which graced many a drawing room at the start of the 19th century. This was a table for many functions. Flaps at either side could be raised to form an oval or round shape. It stood on slender, tapering legs, and the top was decorated with ovals, flowers and leaves of marquetry. These fine little tables are seldom more than 3 feet in width when extended, and at one time a couple of hundred pounds would buy you an excellent example. In recent years a George III satin-

87 Yet another type of English card table, a half-round version from the time of George III. The flame mahogany top has satinwood borders. It is in the £1,000 class.

88, 89 Two examples of card tables from America. The first (88) is a Chippendale carved mahogany table dating from 1760–1780, which could possibly be of Irish origin; note the claw and ball feet with

flattened bottoms to the 'ball' part. The second (89) is from Massachusetts and is 30 years later; it is mahogany inlaid with birch. Both extend to twice the size shown.

wood example hit a new auction record for a Pembroke of £3,900 at Phillips' saleroom in London.

Other occasional tables of the early 19th century, such as the sofa table and the Victorian parlour table, have already been discussed and illustrated. In addition there are the display and work tables. The Victorian housewife often needed somewhere to show off her collection of small objects in a dust-free situation. Enamel and porcelain boxes and silver vinaigrettes were not seen to their advantage in large cabinets, so special tables were made with glass cases forming their tops. Usually these were in the styles of by-gone years, and 19th-century reproductions abound in the antique shops and salerooms of Britain and the United States. For my money, the work table—and its companion the games table—is a much more rewarding field of study. Specially designed for the industrious female of the 19th century, the work table stands on a pedestal, sometimes revolving, supported on castored feet. The lid of the small table lifts to reveal a silk lined work pouch in

which the woman could put her sewing materials. Carving and decoration can be evocative of classical or more recent Georgian days. A similar table with a more frivolous purpose held a compendium of games meant to be played by the whole family together. Pre-dating the Victorian era, and therefore commanding a price almost in the £3,000 range, is the bagatelle table of Regency times, complete with balls, cues, holed board and folding flap ends. When not in use for bagatelle, it can serve as a side table.

Finally, while on the subject of leisure in the home, but digressing somewhat from tables, mention should be made of musical boxes, the larger variety of which certainly come into the classification of furniture in the 19th century. Musical boxes hold many traps for the inexperienced, and the would-be collector is advised to go to a reputable dealer or learn his subject thoroughly before buying. Interior rehabilitation can cost as much as or more than the original price of the box. Splendid cabinetmaking went into the fashioning of the larger

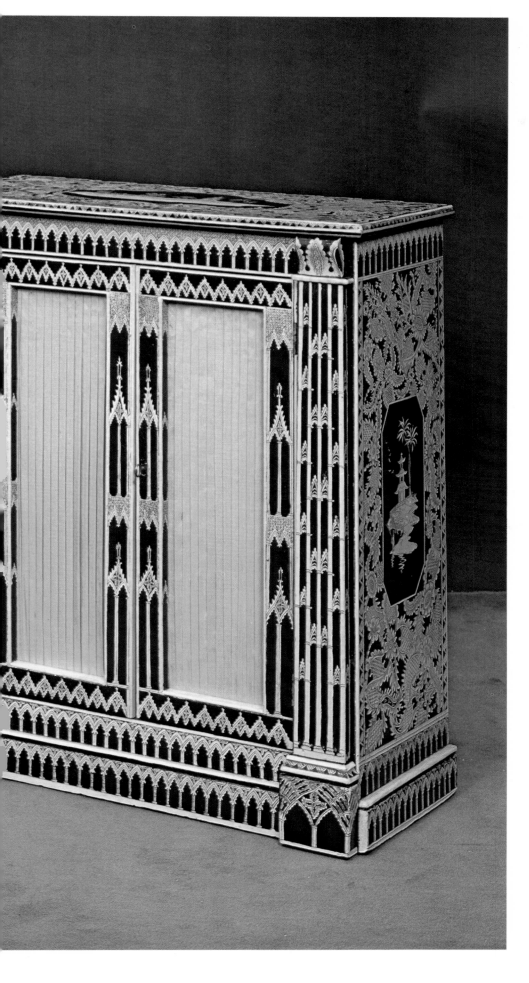

90 Gothic style penwork finely decorates a pair of cabinets made in England around 1815.

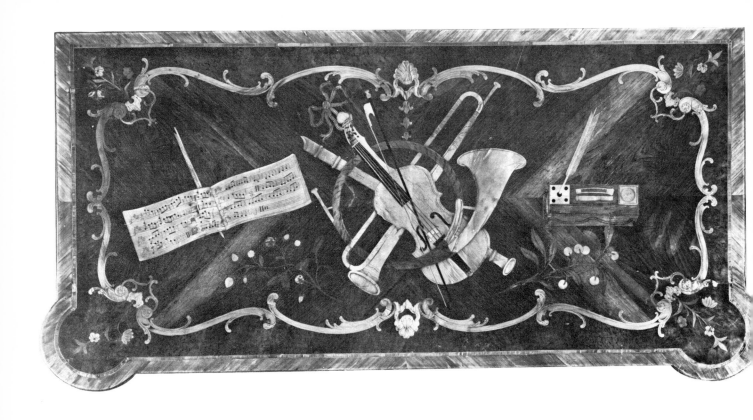

91 Rosewood, tulipwood and burr maple (cut from the malformations of the tree) all went into the veneers which make up the intricate marquetry design on the top of this late 18th-century card table. The inkstand depicted on the right seems to foreshadow a 20th-century design for a portable radio!
92 A George III mahogany oval breakfast table, one of many occasional tables to be found around British and American homes at the turn of the 18th and 19th centuries.
93 This Chippendale walnut tilt top candle stand from Philadelphia, 1760–1780, revolves on a birdcage support. Eminently collectable, but sadly in the $3,000-plus range.
94 From Sheraton's *Drawing Book*, a library table, typical of the intricate designs published by the master.

95 A fine Victorian walnut card table with ormolu decoration. Ormolu (bronze or brass mounts) was often more than pure ornament. It also served to protect the edges and corners of the wood.

96 A George III satinwood Pembroke table. It was a small (four feet when extended) occasional table for many purposes. This one made a record £3,900 at auction in the early 1970s.

97 Display tables were much in demand in the 19th century. This ormolu-mounted example is in the style of Louis XV. The elaborately shaped stretchers meet in a scroll-shaped finial.

98 Typical of work tables to be found in most Victorian homes: the octagonal top lifts for access to the fitted interior in which the housewife would keep her materials and implements.

99 Architect and designer Robert Adam created these chairs in a form known as bergère. They date from 1775–1780 and show French influence.
100 A New South Wales cedar centre table from around 1850 has a marble top hewn locally. Cedar added a particularly national flavour to much Australian furniture.

101 Today they are used as magazine and record racks. The Victorians stored their sheet music in them. Canterburies were so called because, according to Sheraton, a 'bishop of that See' first gave an order for one. This one is in walnut with the slightest touch of inlay.

pieces, and occasionally there comes on the market the barrel organ which was made for home use in the 19th century. Such a gem might include drum and triangle accompaniment and a choice of tunes to be played when the handle on the side is turned. I recently saw a mahogany George II example which, considering its mechanical wizardry, was a bargain at £340.

Music, sacred or secular, was highly esteemed in the 19th-century households of Britain and America. The piano was a 'must' in middle class homes, and most of these instruments can hardly be said to be collectors' pieces today. Despite their modern debased values, some pianos of the 19th and early 20th centuries display good marquetry panels on their fronts. They can be fine examples of the cabinetmaker's art, and it is a pity that our modern living in confined space finds no room for these central features of the Victorian house. Fortunately, an accessory of the 19th-century music room, the canterbury or sheet music stand, finds a ready place in the hearts of collectors. Constructed in a series of racks of turned columns supporting longitudinal strips, the canterbury often housed a single drawer in the base. Thomas Sheraton appears to have been the first to use the word 'canterbury' in print. His *Dictionary* of 1803 says that the name was applied because 'the Bishop of that See first gave orders for these pieces.'

Chests, dressers, sideboards and cabinets

From Britain to the United States there is an export trade in 18th- and 19th-century pine furniture which, while not making a sensational impact on any balance of payments, is nevertheless a steady flow and reflects a basic need of collectors: good quality antiques at reasonable prices. Fine walnut and mahogany having long been beyond the reach of all but the highest bidders, and oak having taken off in price, pine provides the answer for many collectors. The 1970s have seen the opening of numerous shops specialising in pine in London and other major cities of Britain, catering not only for export but for a growing market at home. From the early colonists' days, pine, being cheap and available, was in widespread use by American cabinetmakers. The fact that American buyers now look to England is merely indicative of the rising demand which cannot be met wholly by available pieces in the States.

Traditionally, pine was treated with more respect on the western side of the Atlantic than in Britain. The American cabinetmaker tended to leave it in its natural state, rubbed to a fine patina with applications of beeswax, instead of coating it with paint or stains to resemble other woods as his British cousin did. Therefore at the heart of the resurgent pine trade in Britain we find the business of 'stripping' in full spate. Ironically, the British technique of painting has preserved more pieces of old pine than in the States, as it is a soft wood and highly susceptible to worm and rot in its natural state. Little pine furniture exists from before the 18th century, and most of the antique examples around today date from the 19th century. Thus the Victorian desecration by painting and staining has at least left a legacy of pine furniture to be seized eagerly by collectors on both sides of the Atlantic. Stripping, however, can be hazardous. Over-application of caustic leaves a piece in a state in which a dry white foam will keep appearing on the surface, no matter how much it is treated with antidotes. Careful, persistent application of caustic and much hard work are needed for perfect results. The do-it-yourself pine stripper should take the advice of a specialist and, if in doubt, leave the job entirely to that specialist.

Besides being available and cheap, pine has another quality, and one which earns it a place in this chapter: it embraces the whole field of cabinet furniture, meaning basically that furniture used for purposes of domestic storage or service, from the simple box or chest with a lid to the glass fronted display cabinet and the multi-shelved and compartmented dresser.

The earliest chest was probably a hollowed-out trunk of a tree. It developed into an object consisting of six boards—front, back and bottom, two end pieces to act as legs in keeping it off the floor, and a hinged lid. From this evolved the chest of framed panels and it was not long before the sophisticated addition of a drawer was made beneath the 'box'. Pine was undoubtedly used in Tudor and Stuart England, but it is only the hard oak chests and coffers of that time which have lasted to the present day. The Restoration of 1660 led to refinements in chests as in many other types of furniture, and Charles II's reign saw the establishment of the chest of drawers. By the late 17th century these drawers might have very finely panelled fronts, with brass metalwork and drop handles. It was a short step and a logical one to place the drawers on a stand of spirally turned legs to save the back-breaking work of bending to the lowest drawer. Cabinets with opening doors were also placed on similar stands, which were later to adopt the cabriole leg of fashion. The reign of William and Mary gave cabinets the added lustre of oriental lacquer, and similar excursions into the exotic were seen with cabinet-on-stands through every cycle of furniture fashion in the next two centuries. If your taste is to the oriental, collecting in this field will depend entirely on the state of your pocket. For instance, a pair of fine Regency japanned cabinets can mean £2,000 or more; on the other hand, an example of the oriental cabinets shipped home by British administrators, soldiers and traders in the late 19th century, and manufactured with some degree of skill for a popular home market, may cost you only a tenth of this sum.

Choice of wood for chests of drawers—or commodes as they were called under French influence—followed the general fashions developed over the years, but oak was a common and lasting material for drawer linings. The simple rectangle, the bow front, the serpentine front and the bombé, or swollen, look gave this item of furniture a rich variety in Europe, America and elsewhere. In the glorious years of the 18th century fine panels painted by artists of repute decorated the fronts of commodes made to order for the wealthy. Angelica Kauffmann (1741–1807), born in Switzerland but working in England for about fifteen years, was one such artist whose classically inspired scenes decorated much fine furniture in addition to wall and ceiling panels at the behest of architect Robert Adam.

Furniture designs by Sheraton called for the work of painters of the style and calibre of Kauffmann and Cipriani, whose classical lines complimented his own.

108

106,109,
113
107

110

102 Victorian balloon-back chairs display typical floral carving on the crests of the backs. The frames are in the popular rosewood, seats are of the characteristic 'stuff-over' style, legs the fashionable cabriole of the preceding century.

103 A superb English Regency backgammon table in satinwood, with sliding top. It stands on castors for easy movement.

104 Pennsylvania pine pewter cupboard, 1825–1835, in a style which had changed little for well over a century.

105 The sort of old pine furniture which has soared in price – a New England pine and maple tavern table of around 1750. It is 25 in. high, 31 in. long, and sold for $550 at auction in New York in 1973.

Less than a hundred years after his death, unscrupulous cabinetmakers wishing to cash in on the Sheraton-satinwood vogue resorted to techniques which fooled the gullible. First the faker took a modern coloured print by one of the late 18th-century artists. This he varnished and treated in various ways to give it the 'cracked' appearance of an old painting. From a genuine Sheraton piece he might take a satinwood panel from the side where its substitution by another, later piece, might not be noticed. He would then fix the print to the genuine panel, coating it with boiled-down vellum, and assemble the whole panel as a central feature in a commode or cabinet which was to be passed off as genuine. Fortunately for most collectors, the reputable dealer and the experienced saleroom cataloguer of today are sufficient safeguard against such practices.

The chest on chest – 'tallboy' in England, 'highboy' in its American derivative – is an interesting development which appeared before the start of the 18th century. It commands attention and respect and as such is the target of many a discerning collector. In America it reached such heights that ladders or small pairs of steps were needed to reach the top drawers. The English version often had a pull-out, baize-lined slide of wood which the valet could use when brushing his master's clothes. But it was the American highboy which attracted the most inventive attention and earned itself a place long after the 18th-century tallboy had been ousted from fashion in Europe. The highboy of Rhode Island is a graceful creature of the cabinetmaker's art, with tall, slim lines and deceptively fragile-looking cabriole legs. The furniture of that area eschewed the excesses which marked many of the Philadelphia highboys, with their decorative cresting pediments, often broken in the centre. The craftsman of Newport might sometimes allow himself the luxury of a characteristic carved shell motif on the lowest drawer (found also on some Massachusetts highboys and desks), but otherwise his handiwork was a model of simplicity. Rich mahogany was a favourite wood for the highboy, and for its

112

119

114

106 The full beauty of the age of walnut,
seen in a small English chest of drawers,
dating from around 1725. Above the top
drawer a brushing slide may be pulled out
to act as a surface for clothes valeting.

107 A Hepplewhite rosewood and mahogany serpentine commode of slightly bombé (swollen) form in the French manner. It is decorated with delicate marquetry.

smaller brother, the lowboy, which consisted of one or two rows of drawers with elaborately carved skirt and mounted on whatever were the fashionable legs of the period or region. Other woods were brought into play, as availability and economics dictated: maple, cherry, pine, walnut and any of the basic carcase materials which could be used under the comparatively rare American attempts at japanning. By the early 1800s the highboy was going out of fashion, giving way to lower chests of drawers with bowed or serpentine fronts, not far removed from the styles which were gracing Regency bedrooms in England. Nevertheless the highboy was to remain in the hearts of collectors, and no representative American collection in private hands or in the great museums of the world is complete without two or three examples of these towering glories of the past. Sadly, their prices are commensurate with their stature, and most of us can only admire them in such collections.

The cupboard—literally the board on which cups were placed before they were needed at mealtimes—was the antecedent of a whole range of furniture designed to store utensils needed for the service of meals. Once dining rooms existed in their own right this furniture range grew in variety and importance, and from around the year 1600 change followed change as cabinetmakers echoed living styles.

109 The simple elegance of much Federal furniture is epitomised in a mahogany bow front chest of drawers from Massachusetts, of between 1800 and 1820.

That these styles were running on roughly parallel lines in different countries of Europe is shown by an antique French oak cabinet and a Welsh oak tridarn, or three-piece cupboard. The French piece is a mixture of early 15th-century carved panels, which may have been taken from a church. These have been attached for decorative purposes to a later structure which embodies a ground-level shelf (for pitchers and ewers), an enclosed cupboard (for other utensils and linen) and a flat serving board for the service of meals. The tridarn's three-tier design also allows ample cupboard space and a flat upper shelf area, but has in addition three small drawers for storing implements. This particular tridarn, though

dating from the 18th century, represents a country style which had been in use since the important watershed of 1600. Both pieces, the hybrid French and the pedigree Welsh, are a development from the 16th-century court cupboard (French *court* – short), which began as a set of three open shelves, with plain board backing and standing on bulbous feet. In turn, succession was to go to the queen of the country dining room, the dresser, as popular and as lasting as the Windsor chair. Dresser styles vary from area to area of Britain and the States, but basically the conception is one of cupboards in the lower part, surmounted by a row of drawers. A flat surface above the drawers forms a useful platform for

124

110 Around 1785 Swiss artist Angelica Kauffmann painted scenes on this semicircular commode. She worked in England for some 15 years and contributed classical scenes to much furniture and architectural interiors.

111 A gentleman's cylinder front bureau in substantial mahogany, dating from the end of the 18th century. When the writing slide is pulled out, the action 'rolls up' the cylinder front and reveals a nest of drawers and pigeonholes. To complement the bureau, a Hepplewhite style mahogany elbow chair with carved shield-back.

112 The famous American highboy, this time in cherry and maple. Note the extremely slender cabriole legs in use around the middle of the 18th century. This highboy was made in Newport, Rhode Island.

113 From Salem, Massachusetts, comes a classical carved mahogany bow front chest (1815–1825).

114 Another flat top highboy. Made in Massachusetts, it is in maple, and the brass escutcheons on the drawers were probably imported from England. Popular in America was the shell motif on the lowest, central drawer.

115 Sheraton's influence lasted until long after his death, and this satinwood lady's writing desk of the early 19th century embodies features which were inspired by his *Drawing Book*. Its rectilinear elegance is typical, as is the silk-lined fire screen which rises from the back.

116 A late 19th-century mahogany cylinder front desk on cabriole legs. In 1970 such a desk would sell at auction for around £100. Its price trebled four years later.

117 In a typical saleroom setting (at T.R.G. Lawrence & Son, Crewkerne, Somerset) is seen a late 19th-century French desk of small proportions and attractive appearance. Prominent also is one from a set of four rosewood elbow chairs.

118 A very fine William and Mary
lacquered mirror. It has scrolled paperwork
decoration and exquisite panels of
Chinoiserie, and dates from about 1700.

119 Similar to the elaborately topped Philadelphia highboys is this bonnet top specimen in walnut from Massachusetts, of around 1750. It has swan-neck cresting, urn and flame finials and shell-carved lower drawer.

120 An antique French oak cabinet incorporates early 15th-century panels carved with saints. The sides of the middle section display linen-fold panelling, which suggest that at one time this part belonged to a simple chest for the storage of linen.

121 The famous Welsh oak tridarn, or three-piece cupboard. Note that the upper part has free-standing column fronts.

the carving of meat or the arranging of dishes, and above this is a series of plain-backed shelves running the length of the dresser and on which can be displayed china or plate.

The sideboard table itself grew out of the sideboard of Charles II's time, a long low set of three drawers with a flat-topped working surface, the whole being on bulbous supports with stretchers similar to those found on oak refectory tables of the mid 17th century. Various permutations of furniture design affected the English sideboard in the now familiar pattern: walnut gave way to mahogany, classical replaced Rococo, cabriole legs on claw and ball feet had their day and then surrendered to tapering legs. Adam, Sheraton and others contributed many and sometimes bizarre touches to the sideboard, and by the end of the 18th century it had settled down into a fairly typical pattern: side cupboards flanked a central drawer; tapering legs on spade feet supported this structure, there being four legs at the front and two at the back; a gentle bow front would be decorated with limited marquetry of flowers; and the handles would be simple brass rings. Regency England saw the flanking cupboards lengthened to almost floor-length pedestals. In contrast, a Philadelphian sideboard of 1810–1820 has a deepened centre section formed by the addition of a third cupboard under the central drawer. It achieves symmetry and harmony, two qualities worth noting before turning to the sideboards of the early Victorians. Symmetry there is, in massive proportions, in the constructions which filled the wall of the Victorian dining room. Harmony, alas, is all too seldom present. Even if there was less emphasis on the wine bottle which had inspired Sheraton and Adam to build in elegant cellarettes, the over-fed Victorian householder demanded huge services of china and sideboards big enough to carry this load. Thus the sideboard grew to monumental proportions, and decoration kept grotesquely apace. In later Victorian days reason prevailed, and the sideboards—now needed for a mass market—were on less ample lines.

Perhaps the most fantastic sideboard of the mid 19th century, and one which epitomises fine skills allied to Victorian sentiment and doubtful taste, is the Kenilworth Sideboard, made in Warwick, then the centre of a great school of carving. More like a building than a piece of furniture—indeed, it would entirely fill an average room in a modern house—it is a mass of carved scenes of Queen Elizabeth I's arrival at Kenilworth Castle and of other incidents in her life. Every inch of its Cinemascopic vastness is covered with history in relief, a quality which must have endeared this monstrosity to the Victorians who demanded that every picture tell a story. It is said to have been carved from one huge oak tree in the grounds of Warwick Castle, in a room of which it now stands.

109

122 Visitors to an auction room on viewing day will usually find a fascinating collection of furniture of different styles and periods assembled together, as in this setting at the salerooms of Phillips in Knowle, Warwickshire, eight miles from Meriden, said to be the exact centre of England.

123 The long-neglected English Edwardian display cabinet, seen here in mahogany and fruitwood with classical inlay, has now come into its own. An attractive piece of furniture and rising steadily in price.

124 An early 18th-century oak dresser, of a type often found in pine. This one has a particularly attractive undertier, but the back boards have been replaced by later panels of lighter colour.

125 An inlaid mahogany bow front sideboard from Philadelphia, of 1810–1820. It has a typical arrangement of legs—four at the front and two at the back, a style much used in England.

A similar sideboard by the Warwickshire carvers was commissioned by the county of Warwick as a present to Queen Victoria in 1857. Today it is in Charlecote Park in that county. John Ruskin, who should have known better, said of the sideboard: 'It is indeed worthy of Michelangelo.' Unfortunately, they forgot to ask Victoria whether she would accept the piece, and when it was offered she refused it. Which shows that the queen, when not amused, showed a little more discrimination than some of her subjects.

As none of these large sideboards is likely to be on an average collector's list, we can safely move on to one other aspect of cabinet furniture—the display cabinet, which is as useful today as it was to the 19th-century housewife. Today, a handsome cabinet is the perfect setting for a collection of china or silver, and so the antiques boom in small collectable articles has put a premium on this piece of furniture. It was Mary, the wife of William of Orange (himself responsible for so many developments in English furniture style) who brought from the Netherlands the fashion for collecting porcelain. The Dutch had for some time been proud of their earthenware collections, small and delicate objects needing storage and display facilities. With the growth of the Eastern trade, Chinese porcelain was added to the collections. Ladies at the English court were quick to emulate their new queen, and presently London craftsmen were making simple cabinets with glazed fronts for display purposes. By mid Georgian days China cabinets were offering more scope to the designer, and glass was used for the sides as well as the front. The taste for things oriental often placed a pagoda top on the cabinet, and tracery on the glass echoed the successive fluctuations in style, such as the Eastern, the Gothic and the classical.

A large range of display cabinets was offered to the prosperous middle classes of the 19th century. Elaborate ormolu-mounted cabinets in Rococo style contrasted with simple corner pine cabinets with glass doors. The former might cost you £1,000 or more in an antiques shop, the latter no more than £50 to £100. Excellent country-style corner cabinets were made in the 19th century in America, often mounted on drawers and enclosed lower cupboard. Pine, tulipwood, cherry and maple were used. Although already feeling the touches of inflation, these local country cupboards are among the best bargains in American antiques today.

For long neglected, British Edwardian furniture—a mere 70 years old at its most venerable—has now entered the saleroom and antiques dealing scene. Unfortunately much was destroyed in the inter-war years when it was completely out of fashion, and being of illegitimate derivation it is still frowned upon by the purists who recognise nothing after the lamented death of Thomas Sheraton. Nevertheless, an Edwardian one-piece display cabinet, on slender sabre legs and with tall angular lines crowned by a broken pediment, is of style and size to fit a modern living room. There was a time when most middle class homes in Britain had a similar cabinet. As the man in the corner antiques shop said, 'In those days you couldn't give them away.' Fashions change, and yesterday's rejects become collectable today. Now such a cabinet fetches a figure well into the hundreds.

113

Desks and bookcases

Bookcases and Escritoires, Secretaries or Bureaux, are extremely useful for holding books, keeping papers, or writing on; and, therefore, no cottage parlour ought to be without one.

J. C. Loudon
Encyclopaedia of Cottage, Farmhouse and Villa Architecture and Furniture, 1833

Literate man arrived late in the history of furniture. The basic needs of eating, sitting, sleeping, storage and display encouraged cabinetmaking crafts which were well established and highly skilled by the time literacy spread beyond a relatively small group of clerics and scholars. Consequently the design and manufacture of furniture to assist writing and reading benefited from this heritage, thus offering the most fascinating—and often the most expensive—opportunities to the collector of antique furniture. Desks, bureaux, secrétaires, secretaries, écritoires, scrutoirs, scriptors . . . Call them what you will, they all started with a box, as did the bookcase. In the Middle Ages a desk was an oak box with a hinged lid which allowed the scribe to write on the closed top and keep his materials in the box. Similarly, the first piece of furniture for book storage was the bible box, the good book being the only reading matter in most households of distinction. Early bible boxes, sometimes plain, sometimes decoratively carved, are rare and costly today.

Portable desks continued to be made, reaching high sophistication towards the end of the 18th century. They were useful objects around the house and for travelling. Brass-bound mahogany examples were very popular throughout the 19th century and into our own century. There are literally thousands around. They usually open in two halves to provide a continuous lined writing surface, and they contain an interesting nest of compartments for ink, pens and paper. They make an excellent subject for the modest collector and can often be picked up for a few pounds when needing restoration to locks or lining. Because of their size and convenience, these portable desks were much used by naval officers, who would attach a brass plate bearing their name, rank and name of ship. Keen watching of auction catalogues or commissions left with dealers will lead to their discovery from time to time. They come somewhat dearer than plain boxes, but a quick check with the Navy Lists in London or Washington will provide the lucky buyer with instant provenance. Such a find—a writing desk belonging to a lieutenant aboard an early 19th-century English frigate—prompted a friend to collect over the years an assortment of objects apertaining to that ship: letters, Admiralty documents, books, models and weapons.

The box of old underwent swift changes in the 17th century. It was placed on legs, spirally turned or baluster-shaped, the entire under part following the fashions of contemporary tables. Drawers were added beneath the writing section, and towards the end of the

126 Portable furniture: a George III mahogany table bureau, with tambour or roll front, fitted interior and small drawer.

127 A good George I walnut bureau in two sections. The top contains an architectural, fitted interior and two small drawers. Below it are three larger drawers.

128, 129 Examples of the 18th-century bureau cabinet which illustrate the use of right and wrong proportions. The first (128) is probably Dutch provincial, and its upper part has an unbalanced, truncated look. The second (129) is English, of well-balanced design.

130 An aristocrat of English 18th-century furniture, the Hepplewhite secrétaire bookcase, with swan's-neck pediment above. Tracery on the glass is in the Gothic style.

17th century it had assumed the form of the bureau— three or four levels of drawers surmounted by a top section with fall front which provided the writing surface. It is a formula still followed by furnituremakers of the present day. Enclosed by the fall front were pigeon-holes and drawers. At a touch, buttons would reveal the existence of secret drawers, some of which have given lucky buyers a windfall of gold coins hidden for many years.

It was a logical step to utilise the flat top of the bureau by placing on it a double-doored cabinet. Such a piece was the ancestor of the famous English bureau bookcase which was to reach its crowning glory under Chippendale, Hepplewhite and Sheraton. Bureau cabinets were usually in fine figured walnut, sometimes in other woods japanned. The more elaborate pieces had carved projections at the top and each corner, others a pediment, or gable-like, top which would be broken in the middle. In the second quarter of the 18th century, when mahogany had taken over as the popular wood, some examples had a single cabinet door, instead of two. The addition of the third section called for the exercise of skill and care in proportioning. The later masters, with their fine eye for balance, achieved miracles of proportion in their cabinetmaking. The efforts of less skilled craftsmen, however, led to some unfortunate results which gave their bureau cabinets either a top-heavy or a truncated look. Absence of finer proportions can mean a difference of several hundred pounds in the price of a bureau cabinet or bookcase, and the collector with limited money to spend is sometimes forced to sacrifice aesthetics while nevertheless acquiring an object which meets all the other requisites such as age, craftsmanship and rarity.

Take two examples of an 18th-century bureau cabinet which appeared in different London salerooms within a short time of each other. In form they are similar in many respects, each having four drawers surmounted by the fall front and two-door cabinet. In addition each has a double dome at the top. One is in walnut, stands on bracket feet and displays the tall, elegant appearance essential to the English bureau cabinet, in which the proportions between upper and lower sections must be just right. The other is in burr yew wood—selected from the malformations of the tree for its visual effect—and stands on bun feet. It is early 18th-century and probably of Dutch provincial origin. And here it starts to go wrong: the upper section is too short, giving it a squat look, missing entirely the fine proportions achieved by the other example. Indeed, the catalogue entry for this item read: 'The cabinet-making is unusually naive which may explain the truncated appearance of the upper part.' Nevertheless, it remains an interesting piece, not least from the unusual choice of yew for the wood, which is employed not only in the exterior and interior, but also

131 The davenport, which began life as a portable writing desk, developed architecturally and mechanically in Queen Victoria's England. This walnut example has a top section which rises smoothly at the press of a button and a writing slope which slides out when the cylinder front is opened.

131 The davenport, which began life as a portable writing desk, developed architecturally and mechanically in Queen Victoria's England. This walnut example has a top section which rises smoothly at the press of a button and a writing slope which slides out when the cylinder front is opened.

furniture to acquire, and good 18th-century examples mean an outlay of several thousands of pounds. Late 18th-century bureau bookcases in simple, undecorated mahogany can still be obtained for under £1,000, as can 19th-century pieces. But even here the old story comes up again, and the boom in antiques has already forced fairly late examples beyond the reach of all but the dedicated rich.

If the bureau bookcase was to be found in the library of the man of affairs, the kneehole desk was a 'must' in his study. This desk, with several variations, remained popular through the 19th century and to this day. In its simplest form it is represented by a top section of three drawers, surmounted by a leather lined writing surface and placed on two pedestals of drawers, with a convenient hole for the knees. Variations include a kidney shape, or perhaps a small cupboard for additional storage in the knee recess. Often they appear to be small for modern purposes, more practical use being obtained from Victorian, or even later, pedestal desks of medium size in oak or pine.

Writing desks for women—or 'ladies' as saleroom

for the drawer linings. The different woods and origins of these two bureau cabinets would, incidentally, make price comparisons irrelevant.

Not unlike the tallboy and the American highboy was the secrétaire tallboy chest in which a gentleman could combine storage of clothes and the exercise of writing. Basically a chest on chest of drawers, this item of furniture had in the lower half a narrow fall front in place of the top drawer. Again this fall front would open to reveal the multi-purpose nest of compartments and small drawers.

23, 130   The aristocrat of furniture, however, must be the bureau bookcase, which has attracted the greatest of cabinetmaking skills. While working at his bureau, the gentleman would often need access to his books. The bureau cabinet filled this need. Then, with the use of glazing instead of wooden doors, the opportunity was provided to display his fine volumes. The bureau bookcase which evolved allowed the full play of most aspects of style which emerged in the 18th century. Tracery on the glass doors follows the curvilinear, the rectilinear, the Gothic, the Chinese, according to the whims of the maker and the dictates of contemporary fashion. Bureau bookcases are among the most satisfying pieces of

132 Patently masculine, yet stylishly befitting the man of affairs of Georgian England, a kidney-shaped mahogany kneehole desk from the early 1800s. Note its heavy, moulded plinth.

133 Another Victorian walnut davenport, with fretted gallery. Origins go back to an order placed by a Captain Davenport in the 1790s.

catalogues know them—have attracted the ingenuity of the cabinetmaker for over two centuries. Sheraton produced some excellent designs of pieces on elegant tapering legs. The main section contains a drawer with a flat topped writing surface, backed by shallow drawers and an open shelf. Often the uppermost part could be lifted off by means of a long curved wooden or metal handle, and in this form the furniture is called a cheveret. Elsewhere we find it termed 'bonheur du jour', implying that the woman of the house used it at her first tasks in the morning, such as writing out menus and answering correspondence. Sheraton's influence in these items of furniture shone like a beacon through many of the excesses of 19th-century cabinetmakers, and the bonheur du jour was popular until ousted by the davenport.

The introduction of the tambour or roll top desk gave further scope. A Hepplewhite design in satinwood has a tambour top above a frieze of shallow drawers, the whole standing on fluted, tapering legs. Wide slides may be pulled out at the sides to hold books or papers. A Sheraton satinwood, tambour fronted desk with drawers and folding doors below, inlaid with arabesque

foliage, sold at Christie's in 1904 for the incredible sum of £47 5s. Sheraton, incidentally, called the tambour 'cylinder'. Many cylinder front desks were made in the Sheraton and the French styles in the late 19th century and, pedigree apart, are acceptable 'antiques' at reasonable prices. Such desks have the merit of being small and are therefore in demand. Many of these late Victorian reproductions saw a return to the cabriole leg from the reign of another queen, Anne.

The origins and form of the small writing desk known as the davenport were briefly discussed in the chapter on oak. These popular features of Victorian furnishing were described by a contemporary observer (the inevitable J. C. Loudon) as 'very useful articles for industrious young ladies'. Although their existence is known in the late 18th century, davenports do not appear in any important guide books of the Regency period. Possibly they were not considered important enough by such designers as George Smith and Thomas Hope, who otherwise covered wide ground in furniture. By the time of the Great Exhibition of 1851, however, several firms exhibited them. Perhaps that was the highwater mark for the davenport. Late Victorian embellishments robbed it of its dignity (one designer somehow managed

117

7

to incorporate cabriole legs and serpentine front). Nevertheless, some of these late 19th-century degenerations provide interesting collecting material for the student of the unusual. A furniture catalogue of 1898 advertises these ornate specimens in mahogany, walnut and inlaid rosewood at prices ranging from £1 18s. 6d. to £4 15s. 0d.! The davenports illustrated here could not be obtained unless the buyer is ready to go into the £300 to £400 bracket, although the wide variety available—including some attractive ebonised Edwardian examples—goes down to a fraction of that amount and allows the smaller pocket a chance. Davenports are, in fact, one of the most rewarding fields for the collector of the 19th century. Judging from their appreciation form over the past few years, to buy now cannot help but be a good investment. At the same time, the buyer is acquiring an item of old furniture which will give pleasure as well as service.

The American desk developed from the box in similar ways to the English. Probably the first American mention of a desk, meaning a box with lid, was in an inventory at Plymouth in 1644; there was a reference to '1 little Desk' priced at one shilling. As other inventory entries for desks later in the century go as high as £1 it is assumed that this was a plain pine box. The slant-front, atop drawers, was late in arriving, trailing its English counterpart by half a century. Once it was established, however, the bureau made its appearance in local woods and local styles such as the traditional Rhode Island block front, whose shell carving was to be found elsewhere in the Colonies. Among the best-known exponents of the block or 'sweld' fronts are John Goddard, who lived from the 1720s to 1785, and John Townsend, who died in 1809. The secretary characterised itself in the Salem area of Massachusetts with a projecting centre section containing a kneehole, over which was a drop writing surface. Above this was the glass fronted shelving of an English bureau bookcase.

Bookcases in themselves present a dilemma for the collector. The architectural masterpieces of the 18th century are far too big for anyone without an ancestral hall in which to house them. At the other end of the size scale, the exquisite revolving bookcases of the Regency period are prohibitive in price. Echoing the problem of all book lovers, Samuel Pepys wrote around 1666 that his books were 'growing numerous and lying one upon another'. His is the first recorded instance of a moveable bookcase, as distinct from the fixed shelves built into the libraries of that time. He recorded that he ordered sets made of richly carved oak, and they are now in Magdalene College, Cambridge, housing the Pepys library. For most of the 18th century, however, bookcases were massive creations, not far removed in essence from the wall-filling fixed shelving.

Some diminution in size came with the breakfront

134 Hepplewhite designed this mahogany breakfront bookcase to infuse elegance into massiveness. It has a broken pediment above. The design of the breakfront in three

sections was demanded to control the pediment, which otherwise would have risen to impractical heights, as bookcases became longer.

135 The shell motif, seen before on Colonial and Federal furniture (see 114, 119), appears again on this Georgian American mahogany bureau.

bookcase, so called because the central of three sections 134 protruded. Even so, it was a hefty piece of furniture which would dwarf the average modern room. Below were to be found wooden-doored cupboards, above, shelves enclosed by glass. As the 18th century drew to a close, the bookcase became lighter, and satinwood complemented mahogany as a choice of wood. Obviously, the contribution of the bureau bookcase should be borne in mind in the context of bookcases in general, and as we know, these were splendid creations whose proportions would grace any modern room. The smaller Regency bookcases began to sport plain glass instead of glass patterned by tracing bars. In Regency times some elegant open bookcases were produced with brass trelliswork sides to the shelves; in other types this trellis would form the panels of the enclosing doors.

If your taste is towards the revolving bookcase and you cannot find the thousands needed for a Regency example, I suggest you seek one from the later 19th century, a highly acceptable piece of occasional furniture in mahogany or rosewood. They are normally square-shaped, standing about 2 feet 6 inches in height, and have multiple shelves for books of different sizes. Some contain a small cupboard and maybe a drawer or two. They can, of course, function as coffee tables.

And so to bed

Inventories of the contents of large European houses four hundred years ago reveal an apparent sparseness of furnishings, and this is confirmed by contemporary paintings of Italian palaces. Admittedly, riches abound in the form of carved and gilded ceilings, frescoed walls hung with fabrics from Genoa and Lucca, and a wealth of silver, bronze and gem-studded artifacts. But furniture is reduced to the merest essentials. A bedroom fit for a king would hold only a bed, a single gilt chair, a marble-topped table and possibly a *cassone*, or chest, for storing linen. The bed, however, was a massive, canopied structure, dominating the chamber. Four-poster, canopied beds, in which the sleepers enclosed themselves unhealthily by heavy curtains, were an important feature of Elizabethan mansions and through succeeding centuries. East coast America took to the four-poster with enthusiasm after 1750, but it was hardly a style which recommended itself to a nation on the move: few pioneers had the space or the inclination to take a four-poster with them in the covered waggon. Similarly, today the exploring collector can admire these giant relics of the bedroom, but size and cost preclude them as collectable pieces of furniture.

For these practical reasons, once again the collector turns to the 19th century, and the Great Brass Bed. Metal beds were tentatively recommended in England as early as 1833 by designer and propagandist Loudon, but the breakthrough in design did not come until mid Victorian times with the introduction of brass tubing. Credit for making the brass bed popular in America goes to the irrepressible and unsinkable Molly Brown (how often have influential ladies of dubious virtue been the instigators of furniture fashion!). The survivor of a flood, Molly grew up to be a mining camp 'lady'. She struck gold by accident in the 1870s when she threw a pick in a fit of temper, and became the top society hostess of Denver. Her strike-it-rich success story fired American imagination, and her flashy tastes in interior decoration were copied, as was her bold adoption of the brass bed, a symbol of the break-out from the suffocating tomb of the four-poster. Curtains were still used, but the open frame allowed healthier circulation of air, and gone were the perils of woodworm and ticks. In England, Albert's Great Exhibition of 1851 had given impetus to the metal bed, and orders from the middle classes poured in. In 1875 6,000 brass and iron beds were made in Birmingham, and half were exported to the United States. Gradually the canopy top, or tester, shrank, to disappear completely by 1880.

The vogue for Victoriana has jacked up the price of the 19th-century brass bedstead. Until shortly after the last war it had little more than scrap metal value, and many a fine bedhead has been used as a farm fence or gate. In classified telephone directories you will find dealers specialising in beds in many major cities. A superb brass canopy bed with hand etched posts was recently found in Portugal and shipped back home to England. It was made in 1850 for the export market. A London specialist firm, dealing in old beds, tracked it down to its Portuguese owner who was persuaded to part with it. Within a short time of its return this piece of Victorian fantasy was bought to grace a 20th-century London home at the price of £2,000. More modest examples of Victorian beds, still marvellous examples of ironwork and brass sell for under £100. London still does a steady export trade with the USA, this time in restored and sometimes extended beds, for they tended to be narrower in the last century, and a foot or more can often be added to the width without ruining the proportions of the bed. The clean metal lines of these beds fit in with much modern Scandinavian-type furnishing, hence the intervention of the professional interior decorator and the consequent jump in market prices. However, the collector with a little time to spare should watch country auctions where these beds, often tarnished and neglected, come up for sale. They will need a lot of dedicated polishing and possibly repainting of the iron parts, but the initial cost might be only one-third of the price you pay for the professionally refurbished article.

As a piece of bedroom furniture, the mirror has an important place, although its employment in interior decoration has by no means been confined to that room. By the late 17th century, looking-glasses were being used in the design of great houses. The house of Nell Gwynne in St James's Square, London, had a room completely lined with mirrors. A wide bevel, sometimes up to one inch, is characteristic of early mirrors. Those of the times of William and Mary often had ornamented borders of blue glass or were decorated with fine lacquered Chinoiserie. The techniques of glassmaking being comparatively primitive, the glass of the 17th- and early 18th-century mirrors was not as thin as craftsmen could make it in the 19th century, a useful fact to know if the age of a mirror is suspect. The thickness of glass can be tested by placing the tip of a ball-point pen against the glass and judging the depth of the reflection. Such a test is not always infallible as the 19th- and 20th-century faker was a wary bird, but it may help to

136 Elegance in a Victorian brass canopy bed: this magnificent example of 1850 was sold for £2,000 in 1974.

137 A Chinese expert lacquered toilet mirror from the early 19th century. It is in a swing frame, has two small drawers and reflects the elegance of Regency England.

detect a newer piece of glass in an otherwise irreproachable frame and be a bargaining point in your favour when it comes to talking money. Remember, too, that glass was expensive through the 18th century, so mirrors were small, mounted on swing stands to be placed on drawers, and it was not until about 1780 that the full-length cheval glass came in. The art of the woodcarver is seen at its height in mirrors from the days of Chippendale and Adam. The Regency revived the circular convex mirror, more an object of decoration than a practical looking-glass. American Colonial mirrors had on the whole plainer frames than in England, and the glass was imported. Improved technical processes in the 19th century enabled huge mirrors to be built into the backs of sideboards and above mantelpieces. Reflecting glass was placed to advantage in display cabinets and incorporated in whatnots, the better to show off the collection of bric-à-brac.

I have long considered the antique toilet mirror, in a swing frame mounted on one or two small drawers, to be underestimated. It is a splendid example of a small and available antique. Sound, if somewhat plain, Georgian examples are still to be bought even in the major salerooms for under £50, although the 'flyblown' look of the glass may be a detracting factor. Toilet mirrors from Victorian times are even cheaper, of course, but by this time they were being ousted by specially built dressing tables of pedestal drawers and built-in looking-glass. Having said all that, however, I am aware that a fine period toilet mirror may be priced as high as an entire suite of modern furniture, but on the whole the range of quality, style and period reflects an equally wide variation in prices and is attractive to the exploring collector.

137

Faking and finding

There is a style which has been described as 'the Bastard–Spanish–Moorish–Romanesque–Gothic–Renaissance–Bull-Market–Damn-the-Expense–Style'. It refers to the work of Addison Mizner, one-time prize fighter (under the name of Whirlwind Watson), self-taught architect and real estate promoter, whose aim was to turn the infant Palm Beach, Florida, into an historic Spanish town for the benefit of oil and motor tycoons with more money than taste. Instant antiques were a requisite of Mizner's vision and, according to Michael Davie in *The Observer* of London, workmen armed with Daisy air rifles used to shoot at new furniture to create worm holes of 'age'. 'Shoot from the side!' they were instructed by Mizner, who had learned that worms bore at an oblique angle.

A suspect antique, heavily laden with lead shot, is an unlikely pitfall for the average collector, but Whirlwind Watson's techniques illustrate the lengths to which some people will go to meet the demand for objects of the past. Legitimate restoration of furniture – enough to keep a piece in good repair – is at one end of the scale. At the other is downright faking. Between the two lies the most difficult area for the amateur collector. 19th-century cabinetmakers, cashing in on the vogue for 'styles', developed a technique of virtually turning one genuine piece into two by cannibalising. Many an item of furniture has been made up from a mixture of old panels or other units married to carefully treated pieces of new wood. It takes experience to recognise this bastardised furniture and to achieve the knack which tells the skilled saleroom cataloguer or dealer that a piece is 'just not right'. The ordinary collector cannot hope to have this 'feel' for furniture at first. He can, however, take a few basic precautions, such as looking for sharper edges on carving that he suspects to be new, compared with the smoothed edges of old. And remember that old wood shows a mellowness absent in the patina of the newer.

Owing to the vast amounts of money it commands, French furniture of the 18th century has probably been the target of forgers more than any other genre. Ormolu, the elaborately carved bronze or brass mounts beloved of the famous ébénistes, presents a problem for the man engaged in fraudulent reproduction simply because the true ormolu of the Louis kings in the 18th century was fire-gilded. This involved dissolving gold in acids with an amalgam of mercury, the product being applied to the bronze when hot. Mercury vapours were forced off at this stage with deadly effect to the skilled workmen engaged on the task. Fire-gilding, long discontinued because of the mortality it caused, allows the gold thoroughly to bite into the bronze, thus giving it an instantly recognisable colour, richer and more intrinsic than any obtained from gold-leafing or painting. Nothing short of risking his own life will circumvent this problem for the forger, but he has tried eating off the sharper edges of new metal mounts with acid and staining new surfaces of the wood itself with tobacco juice. Some French fakers of the late 19th century were even convinced that sending a cabinet to 'mature' for several months in foggy London would ripen it for what they considered to be a gullible American market.

Dutch marquetry furniture of the 17th and 18th centuries is rare today and becoming rarer with the insistent demands of Italian and Spanish collectors. Suspect late pieces are more common. In late Victorian times, when British demand for marquetry was high, furniture imported from Holland was often composed of new marquetry glued on to old carcases. And when the latter were not available, new carcases were fashioned and 'coated'. This was a legitimate trade at the time, however, and most of the furniture was sold as reproduction with much use of the overworked word 'style'. A present-day leading London furniture dealer of Dutch origin recalls that his grandparents had huge workshops in Amsterdam turning out furniture for the British market, and he still has the original marquetry patterns. He remembers that the supply of methylated spirits had to be carefully rationed out to the french polishers, otherwise they would get drunk and production would stop. This output of marquetry furniture from the workshops went on up to the first world war and even beyond, evidence enough of the existence of large amounts of late marquetry.

There comes a point, however, where economic circumstances dictate the acceptance of the untrue article. I have read, for instance, warnings of Welsh and English oak dressers being made up of matured oak panels taken from old churches. If the collector knows what he is getting, and good craftsmanship has gone into the work, the result can be an acceptable and very attractive piece of furniture. Again, during a brief resurgence of oak at the turn of the century, oak dressers were imported from Normandy, and I see no objection to these dressers, some seventy or eighty years old, as long as their provenance is known and they are not passed off as older English examples.

Methods adopted by reputable auction houses are worth studying, as familiarisation with catalogue descriptions is part of the education of the aspiring collector. Take for example the enigmatic Sheraton, from whose hand, as far as is known, has come no actual piece of furniture existing today. Caution is reflected in the attitudes of three major London auction houses when it comes to cataloguing 'Sheraton' furniture. Two of the houses describe a piece as Sheraton if it is in period and corresponds to a design in his *Drawing Book*; the third, even with the most authentic item, sticks to the term 'late 18th century'. Other auctioneers throughout the world have similar high standards. Even the houses which have taken a more cavalier attitude towards cataloguing are coming gradually into line, with the refinement of trades description laws, growing awareness of corporate professional responsibilities and the increasing discrimination of the public.

Auction rooms are easily accessible places for the study of old furniture. The large and small museums of the world offer the widest scope, but close examination of a museum exhibit is usually out of the question. The visitor to an auction view, on the other hand, is fully entitled to inspect closely and handle objects. He can take out the drawers of an 18th-century commode and examine techniques of the lining and the runners; he can familiarise himself with the operation of the press-button release on the secret drawer of a secrétaire. A wide range of furniture of many periods is often to be found on the viewing day of a sale of antique furniture. Advice, too, is freely available in the saleroom, usually from an experienced staff of people who have lived with fine furniture all their working lives. The specialists and the porters know not only the current market values, but can also advise on the practicality of an article and where to go for restoration work. And if the potential buyer does not feel brave enough to face the quite unnecessary terrors of the auction, they will do the bidding for him.

Apprehensions about bidding at auction are common but unfounded. No one is likely to find himself with an unwanted stuffed elephant or an old master he cannot afford because he scratched his nose at the wrong moment. The average auctioneer is an experienced animal who can easily spot the real bid from the un-intentional. Neither should the mind-boggling sale totals which are reported from world-famous auction rooms such as Sotheby Parke Bernet put off the collector with a small pocket. All salerooms, big or small, rely on a basic traffic of goods in the £20 to £100 class, despite their star 'flyers'. In one year, Phillips, Britain's third largest auctioneers, sold many thousands of items ranging from a teaspoon to a Ming vase at £135,000. It was there that I heard this sound advice on investment from specialist Ken Brendling, through whose hands has passed enough fine furniture to fill a village of stately homes: 'My advice is—*don't* buy for investment. Buy a piece if you like it. If, after a few years, you sell at a profit—which you probably will, all to the good.

The pleasure you have had from the furniture and the service it has given you all that time is a bonus on top.'

All the principal cities and many of the smaller towns on both sides of the Atlantic and in Australia have flourishing auction rooms. Standards are rising all the time. In Britain, for example, some two dozen firms have formed a professional body called the Society of Fine Art Auctioneers (SOFAA), a praiseworthy move which benefits the public as much as the auctioneers themselves. Full details and addresses of all auctioneers in the group can be obtained by writing to the secretary of SOFAA at 7 Blenheim Street, London W1Y 0AS. Members include not only some of the big London houses, but smaller salerooms in country areas. Many of the latter have frequent sales of furniture, as well as porcelain, silver, pictures and collectors' items, and sale day in the country can be an instructive and enjoyable experience. For the collector—native or tourist—who appreciates a bit of history, good food and ale as well as fine furniture, I thoroughly recommend a sale day visit to King & Chasemore, set in the beautiful Sussex countryside at Pulborough, near the south coast of England. Take a lunchtime break at the 15th-century Oddfellows Arms, a few hundred yards through the village. Should your lot come up in the afternoon, however, I urge you to leave your bid with a porter: the inn, with its superb centrally placed ingle nook fireplace, its fine oak settles, its steak and kidney pie, roast duckling and good ale and wine, can be persuasive and detaining. No doubt many another saleroom can boast similar nearby amenities where the collector can celebrate the acquisition of an auction bargain in style.

While auction rooms play an important role, it is, however, the furniture dealer to whom most collectors turn, whether the shop be in Park Avenue, Portobello road, a country barn or a city back street. Despite the bad publicity accruing from the less reputable dealers in the 'antiques' trade, the honest traders—and they are legion—rely on their continuing reputation. There is no substitute for a sound dealer–customer relationship. The professional dealer knows your needs and your pocket and will be happy to share his knowledge and enthusiasm with you. Mutual confidence has been the keynote of business ever since 'antique collecting' became fashionable. And if you think the vogue for antiques is merely a product of our modern times, I can only quote from an advertisement of an auction which appeared in the *Boston Evening Post* on 8th April 1771:

AT THE HOUSE OF THE LATE MISS BESSY WALKER, ALL
OF HER HOUSE FURNITURE, SOME OF WHICH
IS REALLY ANTIQUE.

Acknowledgments

A number of people and organisations gave their help in the preparation of this book. I am grateful to Phillips, the fine art auctioneers, who kindly supplied a great number of photographs of all types of furniture and provided unstinted facilities for study and for the photography for the jacket; my particular thanks go to James Pettifer of Phillips' furniture department for much useful information and patient help, and to Philip Hoare. I warmly acknowledge the assistance of Sungravure Pty Ltd of Australia, and Helen Marshall, Lifestyle editor of *Belle*, magazine for the homemaker, for providing at short notice photographs of Australian furniture. Similarly my thanks are due to Sotheby Parke Bernet, New York, the Press departments of Christie's and Sotheby's and to Mallett & Son (Antiques) Ltd of London. W. Leslie Weller, of King & Chasemore, contributed valuable time and a number of useful photographs, as did many other members of the Society of Fine Art Auctioneers. I am grateful to Ruth Bayard Minasian, of Glen Ridge, New Jersey, for permission to quote from her book *Royal Nursery Rhymes of England*. Finally I would like to thank fellow writers for their help and inspiration: David Coombs, Editor of *Antique Collector*, Alison Brand, Editor of *Collector's Guide*, David Moss, Editor of *Art and Antiques Weekly*, Susan Ward and G. L. Tyne.

Photographs

And So to Bed, London 136; Biddle & Webb, Birmingham 82, 133; W. & F. C. Bonham & Sons, London 95; Christie, Manson & Woods, London 12, 13, 24, 27, 33, 44, 63, 64, 77, 91, 121; Dowell's, Edinburgh 52, 53, 56; King & Chasemore, Pulborough 17, 45, 73, 76, 115, 135; T. R. G. Lawrence & Son (Fine Art), Crewkerne 116, 117; Mallett & Son (Antiques), London 28, 55, 57, 61, 68, 69, 70, 90, 99, 103, 106, 107, 110, 118; Phillips, London 2, 3, 4, 5, 6, 7, 9, 10, 11, 15, 16, 20, 22, 23, 25, 26, 29, 30, 34, 35, 36, 37, 38, 39, 40, 41, 42, 43, 46, 47, 48, 49, 50, 54, 58, 59, 60, 62, 74, 78, 81, 83, 84, 85, 86, 87, 92, 94, 96, 97, 98, 101, 120, 122, 123, 124, 126, 127, 129, 130, 131, 132, 134, 137; Sotheby & Company, London 8, 14, 128; Sotheby Parke Bernet, New York 21, 31, 32, 75, 79, 80, 88, 89, 93, 104, 105, 108, 109, 112, 113, 114, 119, 125; Sotheby's Belgravia, London 65, 66; Henry Spencer & Sons, Retford 1; Sungravure Pty, Australia, and Helen Marshall, Lifestyle Editor of *Belle* 67, 71, 72, 100. 18, 19, 51, 102 and 111 were photographed at Phillips, London, for the Hamlyn Group by Nigel Messett.

Index

The numbers in bold type refer to illustrations